FULL LINE, FULL AWAY

A Towboat Master's Story

James E. "Ted" Wilson

&

S.C. Heal

Cordillera Publishing Company

Vancouver, B.C.

Canadian Cataloguing in Publication Data
Wilson, James E., & Heal S.C.

ISBN 1-895590-00-0

Cover artwork by Wendy C. Mars

Typesetting by Patricia Gunderson

Printed by Friesen Printers,
P.O. Box 720, Altona, Manitoba, Canada ROG OBO

Published by Cordillera Publishing Company
8415 Granville Street
Dept 46
Vancouver, B.C. Canada V6P 4Z9

To all my shipmates
afloat and ashore,
with whom I shared
these experiences.

"IN COMMAND AGAIN"
The author, Captain Ted Wilson at the controls of a new fireboat, built at Vancouver Shipyards for the Canadian Navy, while out on sea trials.

Table of Contents

Introduction

This is the story of a seaman, one of that unique breed of men who from time immemorial, have stood apart from the rest of us landlubbers as being interestingly different. What that different quality is, is always very hard to define, but most people who come into contact with a genuine seaman sense a "something" that somehow sets them apart. Whether it is created by the way they talk, the confidence with which they express themselves, the often jaunty way they walk or carry themselves, the ease with which they seem to facilitate doing things or just what, differs according to the perception of the listener or beholder. But most of us would agree that there is an indefinable something there.

Captain Ted Wilson is one of those men. Of average height, upstanding and a good looking man who in spite of some past illness carries his seventy-two years with ease and confidence as befits a seaman who has spent all his working life around ships, large and small, both deep sea and around the B.C. coast. He started as a deckboy aboard a Norwegian tramp and progressively made his way up the ladder to command in some of the largest tug and barge companies in British Columbia.

I had known of the author somewhat remotely as a result of meeting Harry Roberts, his brother-in-law as long ago as 1953. In those days Harry ran Associated Tugboats Ltd. from a musty little office first near Menchions shipyard and then later up on West Pender Street, on what was then the fringe of Vancouver's financial district. Associated was a management company for a small group of independent tug owners, and Harry provided daily dispatching, accounting and billing services and just about everything else that boats needed in the way of arranging for groceries and fuel, periodical drydockings and surveys, marine insurance, replacement crew and so on. In short a most needed "jack of all trades and maid of all work".

Harry and I got to know each other as the result of discussions over building a small wooden scow of a type that is now obsolescent, and on several occasions met for beer and a sandwich at the old Pacific Athletic Club, where I became thoroughly bitten with the virus called tugboat fever, and nothing would stop in my way until I was a principal some ten years later in my own tugboat company. It was then that I learned just how versatile a tugboat manager has to be in keeping the wheels turning smoothly whether the boats are at sea or in port, and always thinking about how to pay the bills and where the next charter is to come from.

I only came to know Captain Wilson quite recently, although within minutes of that first meeting we found that we had a great deal in common. I came from a family with strong seafaring traditions and had myself served in the Royal Navy during wartime. I had also had extensive connections with shipping and marine insurance over many years, so with my own past involvement with tugs and barges it took no time at all to establish much common ground and mutual understanding, because we both talked and understood the same nautical lingo which is what instantly creates easy communication between men who have been down to the sea in ships the world over.

At that first meeting another aspect became quickly apparent. This man's story was so interesting and colourful in the first place, but perhaps even more importantly it covered a period in modern history starting at the height of the great depression in 1933, through the second world war until retirement in 1983. He had witnessed and been a part of enormous changes in the coastal transportation industry, as both a working tug-boat master and as a principal in his own tug and barge company. He knew most of the men who shaped massive mergers and reorganisations in the industry. Such men as Harold Elworthy, Stan McKeen, Harold A. Jones, Art Lindsey, Bill Dolmage and a host of others, who followed in their footsteps.

He knew many of the marine underwriters, marine surveyors and maritime lawyers both on the Canadian and U.S. sides of the border and as such they came to rely on him for expert opinions and advice in matters concerning marine accidents and litigation. In short Ted Wilson was not only a witness to an unfolding chapter of modern marine history, he was an integral part of that history and as a consequence his story is not only well worth recording for the future, but is equally well worth reading now.

All told Captain Wilson served in three deepsea, foreign-going ships and a further 40 coastal vessels of various sorts from tugs to small freighters and coastal passenger liners. He experienced typhoons, the sweeping away and jettisoning of a deck cargo of logs in extreme weather conditions, a harrowing but successful surgical operation at sea, and finally sustained injuries which more or less put an end to deep sea service and brought about the decision to make his career in coastal service, all by the age of twenty. His career culminated in his appointment as port captain of the huge Seaspan International organization, from which position he retired in 1983.

Captain Wilson took his retirement seven years ago and lives quietly at Wilson Creek near Sechelt, with his charming wife Eunice. They have a small, neat and cosy home with a nice shady garden, which takes a part of their time and they share this with their oversize German Shepherd, "Bud", who quickly lets visitors know who is really the master of the house. Their two sons and grandchildren are spread out somewhat farther afield, but in Eunice, Ted would be the first to admit that she has been his helper and co-operator all his married life sharing the ups and downs of life at sea, maintaining a home to come ashore to, and doing all those things that fall to the lot of a mother raising children, while father is away for sometimes lengthy periods.

Eunice's part in the writing of this book should be acknowledged from the outset, not only because she has a phenomenal memory, but also because she has had a highly practical hand in a number of events in Captain Wilson's career, acting as boat handler up in the wheelhouse and responding to his directions while he worked logs alongside in a booming ground, to filling the role of acting unpaid dispatcher when they were in business for themselves, and lots of other happenings of a similar nature.

This is James Edward "Ted" Wilson's story and I hope readers enjoy it as much I did in co-operating in its writing.

Syd Heal

Co-author

Vancouver, B.C.

Foreword

Being a seaman by inclination and training, I have to confess that while I have made thousands of log book entries, I am not a writer for purposes required in producing anything like this book. This is why I have relied on my co-author Syd Heal, in bringing together all the elements of my story and setting it out in readable form.

My account relates to the facts of my seagoing and towboating experience, while the additional historical material which goes into a book like this, and adds a bonus of extra interest has been the result of Mr. Heal's own special knowledge, and deep interest in economic and historical matters. The fact that he has been a seagoing and shipping man himself with practical knowledge of ship handling, towboat management and many other facets of waterborne commerce has made my own task that much easier. To have a listener, when going through the various phrases of writing this book, who understood what I was talking about as if by second nature, has been a delight, but to work with someone who could craft the words without losing the special meaning involved in the many circumstances of the shipping and towboat business is even better.

Moreover I must not forget my other mentor, Eunice my wife, who has been a tower of strength and encouragement in ploughing ahead with this project, and I know that Syd will be the first to acknowledge that together we have been an effective team of three.

For the unitiated, a word of explanation regarding the title of this book would be appropriate. When Syd asked me for my ideas on a suitable title, he added that he hoped I could come up with something typical of towboating. Eunice and I thought about it, and felt that a life like mine, could be likened to a towboat voyage through life, and the command, "full line, full away" was typical of a command given at the outset of a voyage, after the tug and her tow had cleared the harbour and it was no longer necessary to be on a short line.

In giving this command, "full line" meant that it was now appropriate to pay out the towline to a safe and comfortable distance between the tug and the tow, and bring the engine revolutions up to the ship's economic towing speed "full away", as the towboat, her tow, and everyone aboard settled down for the long voyage ahead.

Equally the final act of the voyage would occur when the tug is moored or tied up at her dock and the engine is no longer required. Hence the final words in this book, "finished with engines".

I hope the reader will derive as much satisfaction and interest out of reading my story as I did in participating in its writing.

Ted Wilson

Sechelt, B.C.

Chapter One

Childhood Days and Growing up in Victoria

For me life started in Victoria on February 12, 1918, when I came into this world as the second son of Daniel Keith Wilson and my mother Kate Constance Wilson. Dad was in turn the son of the Rev. E.F. Wilson of Sault Ste. Marie, an Anglican Minister who had emigrated from England with his family and had established the Shingwauk Homes for Indians in Ontario. Mother, a fourth generation Canadian came from the King family, her two brothers Ted and Henry King being well-known in shipping circles as King Brothers Ltd. shipping agents and custom brokers, in Victoria, B.C.

My parents lived in comfortable circumstances, father being the owner of Crystal Spring Sodawater Company. When the time came for me to commence school they entered me into Collegiate College, Victoria, a very proper English style school where all the boys wore school uniform and a typical peaked school cap complete with the school insignia. A Mr. Muskett was my head master and it was from him that I struggled to understand the three R's that every schoolchild has to master.

I cannot claim to have enjoyed this school as I went from one sort of trouble to another. On one occasion I was sent out into the cloak room for some minor misdemeanour, and after a short while become both bored and hungry, so helped myself to the sandwiches of other boys and enjoyed quite a feast but there were very naturally consequences when the other boys loudly complained that their lunches had been eaten. Another time I was incarcerated in the boys washroom but that came to a sudden stop when Mr. Muskett looked out of his classroom window and saw long streamers of toilet rolls blowing out of the washroom window.

After approximately three years of attending this school, I was unable to convince my parents to let me transfer to a public school. I was doing well in my studies, but I was most unhappy with the disciplinary actions taken against students for the slightest misdemeanor, such as many lines written on the board after hours, or touching toes accompanied by heavy strokes of the cane across one's buttocks.

In 1927 at age 9, I was presented with a set of books for being first in my form, however, I had made up my mind that in some way I was getting out of that school

With the knowledge of most of my classmates, I found a large ugly tomcat and just prior to class assembly put it in Mr. Muskett's roll-top desk. He came into class as usual in his billowing professor's gown, peering over spectacles half way down his nose. He said "good morning" to the standing and highly expectant class and upon opening the desk to get his Bible for prayers got the surprise we were all awaiting.

The cat having had about 5 minutes in confinement was pretty angry and came out howling and spitting, causing Mr. Muskett to drop his Bible and lose his spectacles as he nearly fell over backwards.

We all waited with bated breath and did not have to wait long. He demanded to know who was responsible for this dastardly deed. No one said a thing. He then said he would hold the entire class responsible, so at that time I admitted to being the guilty party.

Justice was swift as I was told to get out to the front and bend over. I got twelve strokes of the cane and needless to say upon returning to my desk I could not sit down.

I told my parents what I had done and that I would not go back to Collegiate College. It was not for me and after they had a meeting with Mr. Muskett, I at last got away from that horrible uniform and the school regimen I detested.

"Butter would not melt in his mouth."
The author at age 5.

At last after reaching the ripe old age of ten, I was enrolled in my long awaited public school, Sir James Douglas in Grade 5. This school was only two blocks from home, in the Fairfield District of Victoria, and I had class mates whom I already knew. For the first time I really began to enjoy school and realise what it was all about. After one year we moved into Grade VI, now in the big adjoining school where I carried through to completion of Grade VIII and entered Victoria High School.

When I was a very small child, I made two pre-school seatrips, the first in the coastal passenger liner EMMA ALEXANDER from Victoria to Los Angeles, and the second to Hawaii in the AORANGI to stay for health reasons with an aunt and uncle for about a year. I guess those first seagoing trips left some impression on me as my interest in ships and the sea started to slowly germinate.

At age 11 in senior school I now joined the Royal Canadian Sea Cadet Corps "Rainbow" and also took on a paper route for the now defunct "Vancouver Star" newspaper, which meant meeting the C.P.R. night boat from Vancouver, usually the PRINCESS JOAN or PRINCESS ELIZABETH at 0700 hours daily at the inner harbour docks. Good luck was with me as my route was on the James Bay waterfront where Ogden Point docks and the nearby Rithet Piers saw all the deep sea ships berthed. In those days Victoria was a far more important port than it is today.

After a short period of being in the area of these ships on a daily basis together with my sea cadet interests, I had now firmly made up my mind that I was going to join a ship as soon as possible and start a career at sea.

"Things are coming his way at last."
The author at age eleven.

At times the temptation was so great for me to go to the piers and get close to these ships after my papers were delivered, that I was late for school and problems started to develop for me again. Mr. Green, the vice-principal whose room was my home room, saw how interested I was in the sea, and was kind enough to sometimes take me for a sail in his own sailboat, and I eventually took him into my confidence and told him I could not really concentrate on anything other than ships, the sea and getting on a vessel in which to serve. He explained to me how important it was for me to finish school, that I was doing well and encouraged me in my efforts.

Seeing all these beautiful passenger liners coming into the outer piers at Victoria, namely the EMPRESSES OF JAPAN, CANADA, ASIA and RUSSIA, the Grace Line's SANTA ROSA and SANTA PAULA, the Canadian-Australasian Line's AORANGI and NIAGARA, the American President Line's PRESIDENTS MADISON, McKINLEY and CLEVELAND, along with the Admiral Line ships, H.F. ALEXANDER, RUTH ALEXANDER and EMMA ALEXANDER for which line my uncle Will Popert was a vice-president, only intensified my urge to go to sea.

During my years in the Sea Cadet Corps from 1929 to 1932 I became a member of their drum and bugle band and worked up to Chief Petty Officer in charge of it, a role which I might add was to be repeated many years later. This corps was named after H.M.S. RAINBOW, one of the first Royal Navy vessels to be stationed in Victoria, and it so happened that in a collection of naval crests possessed by my mother, RAINBOW was one of them. The captain, Commander Tribe had never seen this crest and borrowed it from me to have a replica made which is still in position above the ship's bell on the quarterdeck.

One day another cadet and myself fancied ourselves as being experts in handling sailboats, so we decided to rent a sailing dinghy. The operator of the rental boat agency seemed to feel we must know sufficient about sailing when we told him that we were Sea Cadets, so the boat was rented to us without any further question. When we got under way out in Cadboro Bay, it was not long before we discovered that we knew a good deal less about sailing than we had believed. Fortunately in one way, we fouled the anchor cable of a moored Canadian destroyer which in turn broke our sailboat's mast and dumped us in the water. With this mishap, the navy came to the rescue, saving our hides from what might have become a fatal experience given the currents that abound in the area. They not only pulled us out of the water but towed us and our damaged boat back to shore. Some people might have persevered, but this experience put an end to my enthusiasm for sailing, and for the rest of my career I served in ships and owned boats which always had an engine!

I went into Victoria High School and enjoyed mathematics and geography but could work up no enthusiasm for ancient history, art, French and physical education. All I wanted to do now was build a boat and be around ships, but when Ira Dilworth, principal of Victoria High School, called me into his office and told me that I could not walk across the school grounds holding hands with my girl friend, this was the final straw and I left school at the age of 14.

Naturally my parents were both very upset, my father in particular hoping that my older brother Doug, and myself would go into his soda water manufacturing business. Doug was twelve years older than I and was already in the Royal Canadian Air Force which became his career until retirement as a Wing Commander after the second world war, and I remained firm in my resolve to go to sea. Dad sent me to Sprott Shaw Commercial School but this did not work out. Moreover my two uncles Ted and Henry King were determined not to give me any encouragement to make a career of the sea, stating that it was no life for a nephew of theirs.

I am sure that I was regarded as being a real problem by both my parents, and these two uncles who were so hellbent on frustrating their sister's offsping in his crazy ideas. Nothing deterred me, however, from hanging around Rithet Piers and the new Ogden Point docks, and I frequently went aboard visiting ships, particularly the Empress liners to have a look around and soak up the atmosphere of being aboard a real ship. One day I spotted a large tramp loading lumber. She was the AVALA, and her black funnel with blood red band and superimposed hammer and sickle made no impression upon me. I spoke to a mate and asked if there was a job on board for which I could sign on. He thought there might be and took me to see the captain.

Things sounded favourable, although I had no realisation that this was a Soviet ship. But before the captain and myself could get very far, in strode the ship's agent who was none other than my Uncle Henry King, so that was the end of my first attempt to find my first ship as he angrily removed me from the vessel. It is not hard to imagine his anger and reaction particularly given the horror stories which had for years come out of Russia about the people who went in, and just got swallowed up in that vast land sometimes never to be heard from again. I have occasionally thought just how fortunate I was to be frustrated by Uncle Henry, as once having shipped out on that Russian ship as a fourteen year-old, I might have had terrible problems getting back to my own country, if indeed I ever did get back.

During the last months in school I had worked aboard a little Victoria harbour tug called the DESBRISAY, owned by Art Warren. This little vessel was a steamer about 40 feet in length and she had one main job, which was to tow the city garbage out to sea each day aboard the so-called "honeydew" barge, where it was dumped into the ebb tide of Juan de Fuca Strait to foul beaches elsewhere on the coast or else erupt into the open Pacific. How times have changed. To do this today would rightly raise the wrath of every environmentalist from one end of Canada to the other, so whatever progress we have made in garbage disposal in the subsequent years, has certainly reduced or eliminated this disgusting practice.

My father was a member of a lodge and knew a fellow member called Captain Fraser. By now he knew that nothing was going to deter me from going to sea so he spoke to the Captain who owned a small freighter named the SQUID which made deliveries of powder and explosives around the coastal logging camps for Canadian Industries Ltd. at James Island. I was shipped as deckhand with board and lodging provided but no pay, which gave me a chance to gain experience in summer school breaks. I found this to be a distinct advance over the DESBRISAY and the garbage run, as we travelled up and down the coast making deliveries and from this I gained my first lessons in practical seamanship.

The SQUID came to an unfortunate end in the 40's while I was master in the tug TRUCILLA, having a collison with the C.P.R. PRINCESS JOAN in dense fog off Point Gray. The SQUID sank but fortunately there was no loss of life, although a warning was put out by Vancouver Radio to all ships advising them to be aware of floating cases of dynamite and detonator caps in adjacent waters. We saw numerous cases floating in the fog-shrouded water as we passed Cowan Point into English Bay on our way into the harbour. I found this most upsetting and it brought home to me the importance of strict lookout practices.

Christmas 1932 was probably at about the height of the Great Depression of the early thirties and for many it was a miserable period involving a lot of suffering and privation for unemployed people many of whom had been ruined by the conditions of the time. My relatives and my father managed to maintain some level of prosperity so that when our family, and many relatives gathered around a joint Christmas dinner table the conversation eventually turned to me. Uncle Ted and Henry were both critical of me dropping out of school and by any yardstick they were very right about the problems I was creating for myself.

They had often made their views known about me adopting a sea career even though they recognised that I was even more determined to go, than they were to stop me. They felt they could help me but wanted me to do the right thing and go into a well-respected line such as Blue Funnel, Donaldson or Rearden Smith, with all of whom they had agency connections. The whole conversation became acrimonious when I made it clear that I was not going to go into any ship where it could be suggested that I had been helped by my uncles' influence, and a terrible row developed. I got up and left the party stating that so far as I was concerned the subject was closed once and for all.

I had stood my ground and the subject was closed, but it was very soon after this that I found my first deepsea ship. I went down to Yarrows' repair facility at Esquimalt and it was there that I spotted a super looking ship which immediately appealed to me, but after the AVALA incident I was a little smarter this time and planned my moves accordingly. Uncles Ted and Henry were very well known everywhere around the Victoria waterfront so I carefully enquired with the gateman as to whether this was a King Agency vessel, and whether either of my uncles was aboard. The gate-man consulted his sheet and told me that the ship was handled by another agency, so I knew that neither Henry nor Ted King would be anywhere near her. However, by now the gateman knew of my relationship, so perhaps that is why he let me go and have a closer look at her. Perhaps I had inadvertently used the influence of their name to get through the gate, but if so it was to be for the last time.

I went aboard the ship, a very smart and well maintained Norwegian twin-screw motorship of some 6400 tons gross registered tonnage, which was in for dry-docking and bottom paint and found one of the mates almost immediately. I asked him if there was any sort of a job available and he told me that there might be, but I would have to see the captain. I went into the captain's cabin and was introduced. His first question was to find my age and at this point I lied to him by replying 16. He told me that there was an opening for a deckboy at a wage of $17.50 per month. I had little idea as to what the duties of a deck boy were aboard a large deepsea freighter but I told him I would be glad to have the job, but as soon as he told me I was hired I thought better about lying about my age, and confessed that I was only 14. I thought for a moment that conscience might have killed my great opportunity, but the captain said I could still have the job so long as I could give him a letter of consent from my parents.

I tore home to announce my good news which greatly upset my mother, but father knew how determined I was and gave me the letter I needed. He was very supportive and told me that he knew I would be successful and would make a good captain one day. My new ship was the M.V. DANWOOD of Oslo, owned by a syndicate called A/S Danwood, one of whose members was the captain, so it was with a light heart and a powerful ambition that I reported for duty on board, on January 10, 1933 about two weeks after stating my intentions to the family.

Chapter Two

Bound for Shanghai

I had little idea what life on a deepsea tramp would be like, what would be expected of me and just what my duties would be, as I walked up the gangplank of the DANWOOD to join my first large ship. But I cared little and thought I would just let events unfold as they would. To be sure, I was excited at the prospect of what was unfolding, as this was what had been maturing in my mind for years.

The DANWOOD was of very similar design to the fleet of locomotive carriers owned by Christen Smith of Oslo. In fact she was almost a sister ship to Smith's ship, the BELJEANNE with extra long hatches, and twin diesels the principal difference being that she lacked the special ballasting arrangements and extra heavy derricks and masts of the heavy lift ships. Smith of course is a common enough name throughout the English speaking world, but spelt this way it was not common in Norway. I do not know for certain, but suspect that there was a relationship between Christen Smith and our Oslo manager who was called Danchert Smith.

It was 1933 and I felt very grown up at the age of 14. I was well aware that conditions ranged from bad to worse for a big part of the population on shore, so I counted myself fortunate in now having a job for some months ahead, and moreover it was even more satisfying that I had obtained it without the help of my two King uncles, as I said I would. I knew my mother was unhappy at the prospect of me leaving home at such an early age, but I felt my father was also just a little proud of me for showing initiative in the face of so much family opposition.

I was sent to see the bosun, who said my first job would be to go over the side to paint the ship's shell-plating. This required me to shinny down a hanging rope ladder and join one of the seamen on a plank, and manipulate a brush on a long handle and thus paint the ship's side. I quickly found that I was petrified as I looked down and saw the concrete floor of the dry dock below. Heights were not my strong suit and it looked a long way down, perhaps 35 feet, but I knew that if I fell off I could leave my brains all over the bottom of the dock. The seaman I was supposed to work with sensed that he had a bag of nerves for company on the painting board and shouted up to the Bosun, who quickly reappeared and asked me if I had ever done this before. I told him of course that I had not, so he soon had me back on deck and gave me safer work.

All the officers and most of the crew were Norwegians with a varying understanding of English. I was the only Canadian and the youngest on board, and quickly established a friendly relationship with the Norwegians, most of whom seemed to take some interest in this green Canadian kid, being only too anxious to be helpful and show me how to do things. As deck boy I was at everyone's beck and call and invariably ended up with the dirtiest jobs.

As is usual aboard Scandinavian ships a great deal of attention was given to always keeping the vessel clean and tidy, and the DANWOOD was no exception. All crewmen shared two-man cabins, and each and every week the mate and bosun did a rigorous inspection of cabins, the messroom, galley and so on, and woebetide the man who showed any sign of untidyness at the time of these inspections.

Aside from deck work my first big job aboard the DANWOOD was to go into the deep tanks to clean out the sludge from the last voyage which remained after discharging her cargo of soyabean oil. The tanks were flushed down with high pressure hoses and scrubbed and swabbed into the bilges with a deck broom where the mess could be discharged with the bilge water. It was greasy smelly stuff and it permeated one's clothing and seemed to work its stink right into the very pores of the skin, but it was a job which had to be done and like the other crewmen I turned to with a will.

The ship had orders to proceed to Shanghai following a round of visits to B.C. ports to load a full cargo of sawn lumber. We commenced loading at Ogden Point, picking up further consignments at Crofton, Chemainus and topped off finally at Port Alberni. She was kept fully rigged for working cargo as she moved from port to port but once we had finished at Port Alberni, we finally made ready for our transpacific voyage. Being equipped with twin derricks at each hatch and conventional union purchase gear, unlike the modern crane equipped lumber carriers, the ship's deck appeared to my untrained eye to be a tangled mass of wire rope, rigging, blocks and pulleys all of which, except for the ship's standing rigging, had to be unrigged and tidied away. Being a single-decked ship. i.e. without 'tween decks, the holds looked like huge cavernous boxes when empty, but as they filled up hatches were secured and further lumber was stacked on deck. In those days all lumber was loose so that each board was loaded in place by longshoremen who filled up every nook and cranny capable of accepting lumber.

Every function was labour intensive compared to the methods of today when neat standard size strapped parcels are handled almost as if each was a heavy single piece of oversize lumber. In those days it took longer to load an 8,000 ton cargo which was about the common size of typical pre-war lumber carriers, than it does to load a 40,000-ton fully parcelled load today. Moreover with such huge modern assembly wharfs as exist at several B.C. ports it is now possible to get a full load on board, working from both the wharf and from scows alongside, without shifting from one port to another or at most loading at say two ports as compared to the three to four in my day. Loose lumber was a menace, as it was so easy for a single board to fall out of the ling and brain anyone who was unwary of the hazards. That was also in the days before the hard hat was in use, longshoremen settling for peaked caps, trilbys, or even old bowlers!

Today it is fascinating to watch the efficiency of the all electric rotating cranes which are the favoured gear of modern lumber carriers, and if one takes into account certain ships equipped with roll-on, roll-off facilities it is even faster as forklifts can run off the dock straight into the ship, in a continuous stream that is only restricted by the availability of lumber parcels on shore.

We unrigged the loading gear and dragged oversize blocks across the deck load of lumber, greasing everything before placing it into lockers around the foot of the masts. The deck work was all run by the bosun and the carpenter, who were both fine men whose job was made easier by having a willing and co-operative crew who needed little direction. I worked right alongside the crewmen, and as I have said before, managed to become dirtier than anyone else being the recipient of all

Norwegian diesel timber carrier DANWOOD.
The author's first deepsea ship.

Breaking seas in the North Pacific.
View from bridge of m.v. DANWOOD on passage to Shanghai with a full load of lumber.

the "Joe" jobs, which was certainly the prescribed way for starting all newcomers, helping them to learn fast!

Derricks and all gear was now stowed away or fully secured, deck cargo firmly lashed by turnbuckled chains which spread from one side of the ship to the other, we were now ready for sea and made our way down the Alberni Canal for the open Pacific. In a very short while, the shores of Vancouver Island receded and disappeared in the distance.

We saw a few fishing boats for some miles out from land but once we had passed beyond their limits we saw perhaps one other ship as we crossed the vast Pacific until we reached Chinese coastal waters. The huge emptiness of the ocean and its changing moods certainly made an impression on me and after a week or two at sea without sight of anything one certainly got an impression of great loneliness at times. There was something mysterious about a distant unknown ship way out on the horizon particularly if all one could see were her navigation lights at night. I remember speculating on "who is she, where is she coming from, and where is she going?", and if other crewmen took any interest a remark might be overheard such as "she's an American bound for Seattle". I suppose I could have found out if I had asked the radio officer or one of the mates as ships invariably spoke to each other usually by morse radio communication, but this was none of my business as I had lots of other work to do.

I was not on a watchkeeping routine such as officers, engineroom staff, lookouts or helmsmen would be, so my day started early at six in the morning, with a quick cup of coffee and except for brief meal breaks, lasted until five thirty in the evening. There was never any shortage of work as the bosun always seemed to have a continuous list of jobs to be done, and if nothing else there were always jobs like chipping steel, or painting.

Other than the captain, officers and crew all shared the same eating facilities which functioned on the cafeteria basis and even though we were all in working rig for whatever we were doing, no sloppiness was permitted and if a person was more than usually dirty when he sat down for his meal, the message was quickly passed that this would not be tolerated. However, this was seldom a problem as the Norwegians all seemed to be particularly conscious of the need for cleanliness not only in the ship, but for themselves. I followed their example in a way that left an impression on me for the rest of my seagoing life.

The food was plentiful and varied but naturally was all Scandinavian with lots of saltfish, sweet soups, goat cheese and other items which took a little getting used to. In those days Scandinavian food had not achieved the popularity that it later took on. Such words as smorgesbord were largely unknown to the average Canadian, so while it was a little strange at first, the food needs of a hungry hardworking youth overcame all other considerations and I quickly learned to like it as I became familiar with the different items the Norwegians enjoyed.

My first trip across the Pacific was uneventful, except for my 15th birthday, with the weather being gentle most of the time as we passed through nothing worse than frequent rain storms. As we approached Shanghai we started to see Chinese junks and other local craft, which as I spotted the first I had ever seen, were quite a curiosity to me. Before long I was far too busy to pay any attention to them as the sea became quite crowded with these small craft the closer we got into the broad estuary of the Yangtse-kiang, to give the mighty river its full name. This time I went overside with other crew members on boards to commence painting as the ship sailed smoothly upriver, and while I thought for a moment that it would be hardly pleasant to fall into the river and be drawn into either of the ships two big propellers, I quickly put the idea out of my mind and got on with the job of painting.

Shanghai itself is situated some 12 miles up a much smaller tributary river known as the Whangpu which flows north into the Yangtse joining the main river at Woosung. The mouth of the Yangtse, marked by the TUNGSHA lightship is about 40 kilometres across and is bisected by a large island called Chingmingdao. The Yangtse ranks as China's largest river and is in fact one of the most important rivers in the world. It carries an enormous flow of water into the East China Sea, which the Chinese call Donghai, and when it is in flood it can do great damage to vast areas in the hinterland.

As we proceeded to bouys at Shanghai, we had also been busy re-rigging for unloading, and all the gear and heavily greased blocks we had stowed away at Port Alberni re-emerged. We commenced discharging into lighters almost immediately and this job proceeded for three weeks. The scene on board was quite different to that in Canada, as all sorts of people swarmed aboard to offer their services in making shoes and clothes, much of the work being done on board and it was all impressively cheap and mostly very good.

At last I had an opportunity to go ashore, but before doing so the captain gave me a stern lecture telling me never to turn my back on a sampan man, otherwise they would have my shoes and anything else of value and overside I would go. He told me to be particularly careful about the many prostitutes who flaunted their tempting wares for unwary sailor boys, and added the warnings that if I ever came back on board with any disease that would be the end of my time on his ship. I was certainly very watchful after this talk with the captain and of course the girls that he described were of no interest to me at my early age of 15!

My first run ashore was in company with some other men off the ship, and it was all quite overpowering. As we went ashore past floating river police stations, I noticed gruesome looking bodies hanging from river pilings and when I enquired, found out that these were cadavers fished out of the river and hung there for a few days to permit identification before being disposed of. Life in China in those days was far cheaper than it is today, and it was nothing to see the small bloated bodies of unwanted children floating in the water.

Mostly I suppose they were girls who in the Chinese social scheme of things had little value, being simply not wanted like the more fortunate boys.

I found that a Canadian ten cent piece went a very long way in terms of its purchasing power, and I could buy a great deal. Suddenly my monthly wage of $17.50 seemed to represent a lot of money, but as my "wants" were very limited, I did not buy anything beyond my most immediate needs.

The next time it came my turn to go ashore, it was made clear to me by my shipmates that I was on my own this time as they had other things on their minds. I spent a short time ashore and then came back to the ship, as I really had very little to catch my interest on shore once I had become used to all the crowded life of people rushing everywhere. I had seen a little of the French Bund and the International Settlement, where most of the foreign business firms were located, but for the most part spent my spare time aboard ship, watching the activity of unloading or taking in the passing river traffic.

I took a lot of interest in the different types of Chinese craft which seemed to fill the river around us. Whole families lived their entire lives aboard, occupying a small usually neat little thatched shelter aft, where they all had their meals and slept. The toilet was a simple structure hanging over the stern where they could defecate and drop the spoil into the river to add to the mass of existing pollution so that the Whangpu was in effect a massive open sewer.

After the lumber was discharged, we moved down river to a loading dock to fill our deep tanks with soyabean oil for the return trip to Vancouver. This was by no means a full cargo. In effect it took the place of water ballast, loading the ship down sufficiently to give her seagoing stability. The return trip back to Vancouver was uneventful and was only broken when we arrived off Victoria to pick up the pilot. It turned out that the skipper of the pilot-boat was Captain Benson, father of a girl friend of mine, Amanda Benson, who was quite surprised to see me.

"Where on earth have you been, Ted?", asked the surprised skipper who had no idea that I had gone to sea and had now completed my first trip to China. The ship got underway and we made for Vancouver to discharge our soya bean oil overside into waiting tank cars and the unpleasant job of cleaning the deep tanks immediately followed.

I was given a few days off and was able to go over to Victoria to see my parents, and have a little time with my girl friend Amanda Benson. Naturally they were very pleased to see me but confronted me with one surprise. When the DANWOOD was a few days off Victoria I had asked permission to send my parents a simple telegram which was worded:-

HAPPY EASTER MUM AND DAD, LOVE TED.

Just seven short words. Dad told me that they had received a phone call from the telegraph company to say that they had a telegram from the M.V. DANWOOD and should they read it over the phone. The worst thoughts immediately ran through Dad's mind as he expected bad news and wondered how he would tell Mum. He plucked up his courage and was greatly relieved to know that it was an Easter greetings message from me, but when I got the bill, it meant a deduction of over half my monthly wage. It was not the ship that charged for sending the message. It was the telegraph company which charged for receiving the message.

Incidentally, I had sent a postcard to mother from Shanghai which is still in my possession and that was very cheap compared to the cost of a simple telegram, but these are the things a 15-year old learns from experience.

The DANWOOD moved around from Vancouver Harbour to complete loading at Fraser Mills and lay just ahead of a large five masted sailing ship which was also loading lumber probably for the South Pacific or Australia. The trip up the "mighty" Fraser, as it is frequently called, on a large ship for the first time was interesting and by way of contrast with the Yangtse was rather like navigating a

American liner PRESIDENT MADISON.
The ship which helped the DANWOOD when a sick seaman had to be operated upon in mid-Pacific.

narrow ditch. I had no way of forecasting the future, but as later events turned out, I was to do this trip several hundred times in my later career in tugboats.

Loading completed we set off down river, changed pilots at the Sandheads and made for the Straits of Juan de Fuca and a repeat of the previous trip for Shanghai, which as matters turned out was to be uneventful except for one incident which I recall very vividly. On the trip back to Vancouver ballasted by another consignment of soya bean oil in our deep tanks, one of the seamen went down with an acute attack of appendicitis. The captain and mate in consultation decided that the only answer was to operate, as the very worst scenario might become a turn to peritonitis and a ruptured appendix followed by certain death.

DANWOOD put out a radio signal asking for assistance from any ship with a doctor on board, and a response was received from the American passenger liner PRESIDENT MADISON, which was a good one and a half day's steaming time away from us. The master knew that the emergency could not await the arrival of the American ship, so decided he had no choice than to operate himself. Arrangements were set up for the two ships to remain in continuous radio contact, and I was told by the mate that I was needed to lend a hand, my job being to man the phone between the makeshift operating room and our radio operator and to relay instructions as they came through to our amateur medical team.

The sick man had been well fortified with liquor to encourage a soporific state and when the captain and mate were both ready, the mate without any warning gave the man a very stiff uppercut to his jaw and knocked him senseless. The operation was successfully completed following instructions received from the PRESIDENT MADISON'S doctor, which was no mean feat considering that everything had to be relayed in morse code tapped out on a key, as modern radio telephones were then a thing of the future. The MADISON rendezvoused with us some hours later at which time we took the sick man over in one of the MADISON's power boats and delivered him alongside the liner where he was whisked aboard and placed under their doctor's care. Fortunately sea conditions were perfect for the transfer and both ships got under way again. A short while later we received another radio signal from the American ship to the effect that the operation had been perfectly executed and the man would recover "just fine".

Of course I realise that for centuries ship master's have been faced with this kind of dilemma, many thousands of times, often working with inadequate knowledge and little or nothing in the way of technical medical aids, but in spite of that have achieved some remarkable successes in treating injured and sick crew. Nevertheless this took nothing away from our captain's achievement or that of anyone else who assisted him.

When we reached Victoria the first man aboard, the pilot, told us that our master, Captain E. Englestad and the DANWOOD were famous as the whole event had been widely reported in the newspapers, all of which my parents saved for me until I got home which was to be a few days later.

Captain Englestad had an odd quirk which he demonstrated to me after I was told to report to the bridge by one of the mates. I had no idea what the purpose of this call to the bridge was all about, as I noticed the captain and the second mate talking to each other. I tried to be pleasant as I entered the bridge confines and said "good morning, Sir", touching my cap. The captain replied with,

"Wilson come here"

"Yes Sir" I replied.

"One thing you will understand is that you will speak when you are spoken to and not a second before"

This outburst seemed a little unnecessary, even though the captain's experience as a doctor had no doubt placed a lot of strain on him. However, I realised later that many masters and officers on duty do not appreciate interruptions no matter how trivial and slight when they are engaged in their own duties.

The mate took me on one side and explained that the sick seaman had been a look-out, and because he had now left the ship, I was to be promoted to take his place which meant that I would now go onto a regular watch-keeping rote and learn to take my turn as helmsman. This also meant that there was now a good chance that my friend Trevor Pidcock from Victoria could take my place on the next trip as deckboy, as I had already put in a good word for him with the Captain knowing that Trevor was anxious to give shipboard life a try.

The duties of a lookout man were explained to me so I now found myself six hours on, followed by six hours off watch. My first night on watch standing in the bow behind a canvas dodger was very scary. There was nothing to see, just darkness with all kinds of eerie sounds made by the wind in the rigging and the swish of the sea under the bows and alongside the ship. I found it unnerving and my imagination ran wild, thinking I saw objects in the water ahead when there was nothing but water. In the event of heavy weather, which could put a sea over the

"A common sight on approaching the China coast."
A large ocean going junk under full sail near the mouth of the Yangtse.

bow, one was allowed to stand his watch on the bridge which was far more comfortable.

There was a bell on the fos'cle head which was for signalling to the bridge. One bell meant an object to starboard, two bells an object to port, and three bells meant an object right ahead. Also the lookout had to answer the quartermaster's time signal through the 8-bell system common at sea or get in trouble, as I did more than once, having fallen asleep behind the winch, and being given extra duties as punishment.

On reaching inland waters I did lots of bell ringing, not only indicating vessels and navigational aids but somewhat overzealously, car or house lights on shore. I was soon put straight in this regard when the irate mate told me that I was driving them and the pilot crazy up on the bridge!

Once again the next trip was a third voyage to Shanghai, but this time I had Trevor for company which made it far better for us both, although as I have said before the Norwegians were a superb group of men whom I liked, and for whom I had the greatest respect, but having an old friend and fellow countryman of my own age along, made such events as going ashore in Shanghai just that much more interesting and enjoyable. We visited Chinese theatres, ate in cafes and visited all kinds of shops. Trevor's presence made all the difference, compared to my first visit when I felt real loneliness, aboard a foreign ship in a foreign land.

When we returned to Vancouver our routine was to be changed considerably, for this time the ship had orders to load B.C. lumber from the usual range of ports for New York. By now I was well tuned into watchkeeping and had gained experience at the wheel. The Panama Canal was a great thrill for both of us, with so much to see for the first time, and there is no question that the Canal is one of the engineering wonders of the world. We were both enthralled to witness our ship being towed through the Miraflores and Gatun locks by tiny electric locomotives. Of course DANWOOD was small fry compared to the huge battleships and aircraft-carriers which these small machines handled with almost equal ease.

We entered the Hudson River and made for Erie Basin to unload part of our lumber cargo and after having lightened ship, proceeded up the Hudson River to Albany, a distance of around 150 miles up river, passing under numerous rail and road bridges on the way. The river broadened considerably above New York City and then narrowed into quite a confined stream beyond Peekskill. This was quite unlike any trip I had done or was ever to do again, as we caught views of a cross-section of New England country life with small towns, villages, farms, forests and stately homes and just about everything else on the way.

Albany is the most northerly point on the Hudson for deep sea ships of our type. It is also a pleasant little city and state capital for New York. Sunday was a day off, so Trevor and I decided to visit a local church. We had a black messboy on board with whom we were both quite friendly as he was about the same age as us, so George as I will call him, asked us if he could come along with us. We never gave it a further thought and told George that he was welcome. We walked through the town and eventually came to a church whose denomination I no longer recall and made our way inside.

We were met by an usher who asked us what we wanted, which was a little strange as I would have thought the answer obvious when three young fellows obviously wearing their best shore-going clothes walk into a church on a Sunday morning with other worshippers already there in substantial numbers. I responded to his enquiry by saying that we were here for the service. What he was obliquely referring to was the black boy. He now came out with it directly by saying that we two, Trevor and I, were welcome to stay but George being black, could not stay. I was maybe a little loud in my protests, and it seems likely that someone had immediately phoned the police, anticipating trouble, because very soon a policeman walked in and asked us to come outside, where he walked us to his police car. He was quite nice but explained the problem and the "no blacks" rule. This was still white America in the early thirties and the blacks had won few of the gains they were later to make. Sixty years later that sort of incident would have caused a lot of trouble of a different kind, and been disallowed by civil rights legislation across America, including the State of New York.

He suggested that we go about our business quietly, because if he had any further trouble he would have to take stronger measures. What looked like starting as a nice day ended very quickly on an unhappy note as we made our way back to the ship. I recall a similar incident from my early childhood, when after travelling in the American S.S. EMMA ALEXANDER from Victoria to Los Angeles my mother and I stayed with an aunt for several days. I was maybe about four years old, which would place it as being 1922 and as small children will usually do they quickly find a playmate, in this instance a little black boy about my own age. I went over to his house and after a short while went back home to my aunt's and asked if I could bring my new friend over for "tea", a very usual expression for Anglo-Canadians of all ages at that time.

Yes I could, so I promptly went back to my friend's home and told his mother. She got him washed and tidied up and over we went to my aunt's, who was aghast when she saw my little friend, and I was told that he could not come in, so that little taste of democracy came to a swift end.

These sort of incidents really smite heavily at the innocence of childhood and youth. I had never been brought up to show intolerance to anyone, and in spite of my family's strong views about education and such good old Anglo-Saxon virtues as working at something meaningful, such prejudices never had any place in their lives. So far as I am concerned the same position applies today as there is room for us all in the nature of things, and no one should be prejudiced on account of the colour of his skin.

We returned to Vancouver in ballast to be advised that a second trip was scheduled for New York and Hudson River ports, but by this time Trevor was starting to have doubts about a seafaring career. He was pursuaded to make the next trip which was to be more or less a repeat of the first, except that after unloading part of our cargo at the Erie basin, we were to proceed to another small river port called Irvington to discharge the balance. Irvington was very much an industrial suburb about thirty miles upriver and it had little attraction.

As I spent a lot of time doing my watches on the bridge, I picked up snippets of conversation between the mates and the master. Captain Englestad had an ownership interest in the ship which had already done three voyages to China, and two to New York since I joined her. I got the feeling that they were dissatisfied about this trade and would be making some changes, but of course nothing was passed on to me.

Also Trevor had made up his mind that he would sign off at the end of this trip, but as matters turned out our minds were made up for us when the master spoke to both of us and told us that the ship would be returning to Norway for refit and entry into another trade. He told us that he had been more than satisfied with us both, but wanted to discharge us at Vancouver as going to Europe with all the uncertainties of the time, the worldwide trade depression still being very bad, and with massive unemployment everywhere, we could find ourselves stranded in a foreign land.

We could not argue against the logic of what he said and nor did we wish to, so I for one parted company with a fine ship and crew from whom I had learned a great deal. During my time in the DANWOOD and her trade, I learned a smattering of the various languages around me namely Norwegian, Danish, German, Swedish, Chinese, Japanese, Russian and French but unfortunately I have lost the ability to handle any of them. Eight languages, plus English, could be very confusing!

Trevor left the sea but I already had my name in to join a Vancouver shipping company as a cadet in one of their ships and as soon as I got back I checked with them to see if they now had a position open. I was told that the present cadet was ashore writing his exams and if he passed he would be shipping out again as third mate in which case I could take his place as cadet, and that is how I came to join the S.S. CITY OF VANCOUVER, and thus commence another chapter in my seagoing career.

Chapter Three

Working for Coughlin's and the S.S. CITY OF VANCOUVER

Before going into detail on my own association with the Coughlin interests and my two voyages aboard their freighter, the CITY OF VANCOUVER, my co-author is the source of historic background on what I consider to be a fascinating British Columbia enterprise which is part of the historic fabric of Vancouver and indeed Canada, but is now only remembered by old-timers. At my then young age, I was not aware of this background and references to the Coughlin shipbuilding activities, which were both prolific and important during, and in the aftermath of the first world war. After they gave up shipbuilding, they continued as shipowners until the late thirties, and any memory of them can now only be found in old Lloyd's Registers and odd press clippings tucked away in archives. Beyond that, little seems to be remembered of this important enterprise and today I may be one of the very few surviving, who served in their ships.

J. Coughlin & Sons evidently grew with Vancouver as part of the railway and sawmill age. They were bridge builders, and steel fabricators and no doubt quite a few other things when it came to iron and steel. I do not doubt that their name plate can still be found on old railway and road bridges around B.C., including the historic Kitsilano trestle which spans False Creek. They really made their name in the latter years of the First World War, when Britain being in the direst peril as the result of the depredations of German U-boats on its shipping, came to Canada to develop a shipbuilding program in much the same way as was to happen on a far larger scale in the second war.

The crown agency for placing orders was the Imperial Munitions Board, which eventually ordered eighty steel and wood ships. Of these 48 steel ships were either ordered for private owners and requisitioned by the I.M.B. or built directly for the board. Three steel ships were built by Wallace Shipyards, later to be well known as Burrard Dry Dock Company and eventually as Versatile Pacific Shipyards, and ten came from the Coughlin yard. Coughlin was the only yard to build the 8,800 ton-deadweight class, and in fact these were the largest ships in the British program.

Essentially the ships were typical British-designed three island tramp steamers of a type which were built by the thousand from the later years of the nineteenth century until after the second world war. Naturally as the years went by the design improved and the size increased to about the optimum of 10,000 tons deadweight. The Canadian built "Fort" and "Park" ships of the second war were typical in every respect, except that they were flush decked without a prominent fo'c'sle or poop.

In configuration there was usually a forecastle (always pronounced fo'c'sle) or forepeak, a well deck with holds one and two and the foremast between, which was rigged to work two derricks to each hold, then the bridge and deck officers accomodation followed by number three hold served by twin derricks. Then followed the cross bunker for coal fuel, the boiler and engineroom over which was the engineers accomodation and the single funnel, followed by number four and five holds between which was the mainmast rigged usually the same as the foremast and the raised poop over the propeller. In these ships deck crew usually berthed in the foc'sle, and engine and boiler room hands berthed in the poop.

The British program was followed by an even bigger one initiated by the Canadian government, which harboured ambitions to see their newly organised Canadian National Railways expand into a global transportation empire like their privately owned and highly successful competitor, the Canadian Pacific Railway. Sixty-eight ships more or less identical with the eight different types built for the British were launched for what was known as the Canadian Goverment Merchant Marine, and of these six of the 8,800 tonners came from Coughlin's, although by now other yards were also building this largest size ship of both programs.

Coughlin's were to build several additional ships of the class for Scandinavian and Belgian owners as well as three additional 8,800 tonners, the CITY OF VANCOUVER, CITY OF VICTORIA, and the MARGARET COUGHLIN. All three ships were for their own account although they were registered as being owned by single ship companies, the VANCOUVER being legally owned by the Vancouver S.S. Co. Ltd. and VICTORIA by British Canadian Steamships Ltd. and the MARGARET COUGHLIN by Canadian Western Steamships Ltd. There is no record of the managers of the last steamer because she had been sold foreign by 1925 but the other two were managed, until the shipowning business ended in 1936, by Ocean Shipping Co. Ltd. who had engaged me at their offices at 640 Howe Street in Vancouver.

No matter how legal ownership broke down, the business was popularly known as the "Johnny Coughlin Line" and specialised in carrying outward cargoes of B.C. sawn lumber and logs, mostly across the Pacific to China and Japan, but with trips to such places as Garston, the lumber depot of the port of Liverpool on Britain's River Mersey.

I had put my name down with Coughlin's to join their first available ship as a cadet with the idea of going after my deep-sea certificates and eventually becoming a ship's master. By now I was sixteen and already had five round voyages in the DANWOOD to my credit so I was favourably regarded as having already had a fair amount of deep sea experience. Most cadets, or apprentices as they are called in some lines, usually go straight from school at the age of 16 or 17 without any lower deck experience. While I was what is frequently labelled a school drop-out, I had a healthy march on others at my then tender age, in terms of hands-on experience.

After a brief respite ashore from the DANWOOD I joined the CITY OF VANCOUVER at the princely wage of $35 per month. I had to buy an officer's "fore and aft" uniform, but Captain Malcolm Buchanan, a dour Scotsman if there ever was one, suggested that while in Vancouver I buy an officer's uniform cap with the company's insignia on it, and then buy the rest of my uniform in Shanghai, where from previous experience my few Canadian dollars would go a great deal further. This matter of uniform was important in these ships as it represented a symbol of authority among an all-Chinese deck and engineroom crew. All the officers, consisting of the captain, chief engineer, three mates and three assistant engineers and the radio operator were white. The deck officers had their own saloon under the bridge structure, and the engineers likewise in their accomodation over the engine-room,

"OLD CHINA HAND"
Brass -bound and fore and aft rigged. The author in his new uniform as a cadet in 1934 aboard the tramp steamer "CITY OF VANCOUVER."

while the Chinese had their own arrangements. The Chinese hands usually had little or no knowledge of English so all communication was through the Chinese bosun, which made him a very vital man on board.

On the whole the Chinese were hard working, and reliable and made up a good crew, but the social gulf between white officers and oriental crew had to be maintained at all costs. This was quite in contrast to the democratic regime aboard the DANWOOD where officers, other than the captain, and all other hands shared common eating facilities.

One quirk aboard the CITY OF VANCOUVER which heightened the relative loneliness of being the only cadet aboard was that I ate with the engineers who I felt barely tolerated me, whereas being an apprentice deck officer I should have messed with the officers in their accomodation. I certainly worked with them on the bridge and around the ship, and I know that this arrangement would have not been tolerated in most other owner's ships particularly British after whose system we modelled our operation in Coughlin's. The whole set-up tended to make one feel something of an outcast and heightened the suspicion that cadets, apprentices, or midshipmen as we were called in the Navy, were the lowest form of animal life aboard a ship! At one point being thirsty for some life around me, I went down to the Chinese quarters in the after part of the ship to watch them playing fan-tan and enjoying their other games, but news of this leaked back to the bridge and I was told in no uncertain terms that this was against the rules. Looking back, the whole arrangement of my work, my messing and my fraternizing was pretty ambivelent, and it was enough to give a young fellow a real complex.

I don't remember the names of all the officers aboard our ship. Aside from Captain Buchanan, Mr. Atkinson was first mate, Jim MacDonnell was second and Mr Dobie was the new third. I lost all contact with Mr. Atkinson after leaving this ship, but Captain MacDonnell became well known around Vancouver shipping circles setting up a coastal operation of his own after the war and later going into the manufacturing business. His company was called Maritime Industries Ltd. where he introduced a number of innovative marine engineering projects which are still important today. Captain Dobie was to retire many years later as Vancouver Harbour Master.

The very first time I was given a small job to do on the bridge, could have ended quite disastrously before we had even left Vancouver on my first trip aboard. The captain had given the newly made third mate, time off to be married so we were a mate short for the simple movement of leaving our berth at Vancouver and making for the Moodyville buoys to load logs. The mate would have been stationed in the bow, and the second at his customary station on the poop when shifting ship, so I was required to take the third's position assisting the captain on the bridge, by working the engine-room telegraph. This seemed simple enough except that I had never actually worked on the bridge telegraphs before, only acting as helmsman and look-out.

These telegraphs were of the type in which the lever had to be worked right down and back again to activate the bells at the engineers' control panel in the engine room; then finally placing the lever at the desired command position which might have been "slow ahead" or "full astern" or what have you. In any event the mistake was spotted in response to a hurried call to the bridge from the chief engineer. I don't remember what the captain said, but it would not be hard to imagine him saying impatiently and perhaps a little sarcastically, "Look Laddie, this is what you have to do" in his Scottish burr. Mind you, once shown I seldom had to be shown anything a second time, so the mistake was never made again!

If I thought there were any special privileges for an officer cadet aboard this ship, I was quickly proven wrong. The captain possessed a large bulldog which was his companion throughout our long voyages. Captains tend to live apart and somewhat loftily above their officers and of course never associated with common crew, whether they be white, Chinese or anything else. On this occasion I was making my way up to the bridge and was just crossing the small bridge deck outside of the captain's cabin. His dog had just defecated on the deck so he looked at me and said,

"Get rid of that"

"Yes Sir, do you have anything I can pick it up with"

"I don't but you do. Use your hands" was the captains response.

I thought better than to say anything else, remembering the dressing down I got from the captain of the DANWOOD in response to my cheery "Good morning, Sir". I picked up the foul mess and dumped it overside, after all I had often had my hands much dirtier than they now were.

After finishing at Moodyville, we made our way through the Second Narrows in Vancouver Harbour to the Dollarton Mill just inside Indian Arm to start loading lumber below decks. I was fascinated to observe Chinese crew members hooking jellyfish out of the water and then eating them on the spot. Apparently it was a delicacy to them. Upon departing from Dollarton we proceeded to Port Alberni to finish off our load of logs and lumber. Upon completion we then made ready for sea disassembling all cargo handling gear, greasing it and stowing it away neatly in lockers in the fo'c'sle. The difference this time was that I did not do it myself, as in the DANWOOD where by now I would have been in grease to my armpits. The Chinese crew did it all under the direction of the bosun, I being expected to learn by watching.

S.S. CITY OF VANCOUVER
Looking like a model as she sails into Vancouver Harbour. One of the very rare Vancouver-owned deepsea ships engaged in international trade between the two wars.

S.S. CITY OF VANCOUVER
of the "Johnny Coughlin Line". The author's two trans-Pacific voyages were jinxed by bad weather and fatalities.

The second mate Mr. McDonnell, told me to go on the dock and check the Plimsoll load line painted on the ship's hull amidships. I knew what it was but could not find it and came back and reported to the second. He told me I must be stupid and this time came up with me to see for himself. Sure enough the load line was submerged and in truth the ship was illegally overloaded. No one seemed to be concerned, and in Port Alberni there was no one to check the matter out so we sailed in that condition with only about six feet of freeboard from the lowest point on the well deck to the water. Overloading, deliberate or accidental, is a serious situation and had the ship been lost as a result of its condition, the consequences for both the owners and the master could have been severe.

As it turned out the CITY OF VANCOUVER was not a lucky ship weatherwise, and we were at one point in very dire peril in our transpacific voyage in overloaded condition. When we were approaching Northern Japan on the North Pacific great circle route, we were caught in heavy typhoon seas. These ships supposedly had a designed speed of 11.5 knots, but now could only do a dishonest 10 knots at best, and that was with everything including wind and tide in their favour, so there was no reserve of power. First the heavy timber stanchions which supported our forward deck load carried away to be followed by a large part of the deck load itself, which in turn ripped out our bulwark, and brought down the fore upper topmast and carried away our aerial. Fortunately the captain had a short while earlier put out a distress advisory, telling the world that we were in difficulties and requested a vessel to standby us. The Canadian Pacific EMPRESS OF ASIA had acknowledged and was making for our position. Now of course we could not send out further signals as our condition further deteriorated. I think the ship's condition was more serious than I had believed with my very limited experience, because with the forward deck load having been lost, the ship was now badly out of trim. The captain decided he had no choice other than to jettison some of the aft deck cargo to trim the ship, now quite badly down by the stern. Unfortunately in doing so three Chinese deck hands were lost overboard and drowned, and again the aft bulwarks took further heavy damage.

The EMPRESS OF ASIA made for our last reported position, so it was quite a relief to see her there as she stood by us until the weather moderated and we were able to safely get under way again for Shanghai. That storm took quite a toll of the ship and cargo with almost all our deck cargo lost or jettisoned, and the foremast, aerial and bulwarks damaged not to mention three lives. Due to heavy weather delays lasting several days, we ran short of coal three days out of our destination, so all hands were turned to handling our lumber cargo into the stokehold for fuel.

Tramp freighters of our type deeply-laden, essentially low-powered with minimum freeboard, sometimes took a terrible beating and every year such ships would be lost in extreme weather conditions in the North Pacific and North Atlantic. Interestingly enough, it was many years later that I met Bill Henry, through the Sea Cadets. He had been bridge boy on the EMPRESS OF ASIA at the time of our mishap. When the ASIA responded to our distress advisory she immediately changed course for our position, and there was a good deal of consternation on board when they passed through a sea of floating logs and lumber. They feared the worst and thought that the CITY OF VANCOUVER had already foundered and had become another mystery of the sea.

We made directly for Shanghai, this time going even higher up the Whangpu river than before to a shipyard, where we offloaded what little remained of our deck cargo into lighters. Repairs took about three weeks, but while there I did not go ashore until moving further down river to a berth at Wetmore Road. While in Vancouver, Uncle Ted King had given me the name and phone number of a friend of his in Shanghai, a Captain Redvers Smith of Standard Oil, as I had told my uncle how very much I was on my own when calling at these ports.

In going ashore at the foot of Wetmore Road, I was passing by the massive entrance gates to a huge home and the Ewo Cotton Mills where I noticed an elderly white gentleman sitting under an umbrella talking to another man. I asked the gatekeeper if I could speak to him and seeing me in uniform, the young Chinese boy went over to the table, spoke to the white man, and I was invited in. I introduced myself and asked if I could use the telephone. He said I could and called a "chinaboy" over, as servants were called in those days. The servant took me to a phone where I tried calling Captain Smith only to be told that he had left on a tanker and would not be back home again for three weeks.

When I got back he seemed to notice that I was disappointed and invited me to sit down offering me refreshments. He wanted to know where I was from and when I replied Victoria, B.C., he was not even certain as to where my home town was. Very soon a car arrived and three young people got out, whereupon the gentleman introduced me to his two sons and very attractive daughter. They were an English family called Harrop, the father being manager of the Ewo Cotton Mill where we were now all chatting.

I do not recall the names of the two boys, but "Girlie" as she was called was very friendly and made me feel very much at home, particularly after an invitation was given me to come with them into their home for dinner. This I did, and I must say it was quite an experience, the home being large and palatial by any standard, with lots of servants who served up a fine English style dinner to which I took no objection. The dinner date became an invitation to stay overnight and this in turn grew into the entire weekend. They had two cars, the smaller of which was a Packard, and I did get the opportunity of driving it but was not too confident about driving on the "wrong" side of the road.

I went back to the ship to pick up pyjamas and my toilet gear, and the following day they took me down river in their fast boat to visit their other home at Woosung overlooking the Yangtse itself. I now had a fine family of friends to visit on my next trip, and sure enough when I got home to Victoria a letter awaited me from Girlie Harrop making sure that I knew I was to call again, so I guess I now had a girl friend in Shanghai!

After leaving Shanghai we made for Tsingtao which has a beautiful natural harbour not unlike Vancouver in some ways. Gaining entry is tricky as the entrance is so narrow and involves a nasty right angled turn. On this occasion the weather was bad outside with a typhoon warning up, a heavy swell running, and the pilots not available. Captain Buchanan was not happy about waiting outside or trying to lay to an anchor, so as he had been in and out of this port on many occasions he decided to take her in himself; the understanding being that a pilot would be waiting on the inside.

We entered the pass and it was then, when we were fully committed, that the ship's steering decided to give trouble so this function had to be transferred to the emergency steering on the poop aft. It was a thrilling few moments at a most critical time, but we made it even though the ship was rolling 40 degrees at times until we got into the calmer water of the inner harbour. The ship was of course very tender due to having cargo remaining only on deck and in the 'tween decks.We discharged our Tsingtao cargo and then made for Dairen, a Chinese port on the north side of the Gulf of Korea. Here we cleared out the remaining cargo and loaded soya bean oil in wooden kegs in the 'tween decks, and filled the remaining space with bagged peanuts. After coaling we made for Hakodate Straits and homeward to B.C. in what proved to be largely an uneventful trip, although some soya oil kegs broke adrift during heavy weather and spilled their contents on the bagged peanuts creating quite a mess along with clogged bilges in number two hold. But after the outward trip from British Columbia, who could possibly need more excitement?

I was able to visit my parents again and while in Victoria visited my Uncle Captain "Fritz" Walter who had retired from the Royal Navy and was married to Dad's youngest sister. Uncle Fritz had been in command of Royal Navy ships on the west coast such as SHEARWATER and NIOBE, and was very interested in my adventures. A few days later he visited my parents' home to present me with his sextant.

I returned to the CITY OF VANCOUVER for my second trip. We loaded at the usual collection of B.C. loading points and left once again for Shanghai where this time I had a welcoming "home from home" awaiting at the Harrops but most particularly from Girlie Harrop. I told second mate Jim McDonnell about my new

Canadian Pacific liner EMPRESS OF ASIA which answered the CITY OF VANCOUVER's distress signal. Passing under the still uncompleted Lions Gate Bridge.

Deck Officers aboard s.s. CITY OF VANCOUVER
Standing: Second Officer Jim McDonnell, Third Officer Dobie, Chief Officer Atkinson.
Radio officer, and the Author

sextant, so the first time out, when shooting the noon sight to fix our position, I was invited by Captain Buchanan to join the other officers for this daily ritual. I did what I thought was correct, but the captain said that my figures did not agree with his or the other officers, so he worked through them with me. He shook his head, "the way you have it laddie, you have placed this ship right in the front pew of Christchurch Cathedral, Victoria!". I suppose being such a kid in reality, even though I sometimes felt very grown up, I was the subject of some mild amusement at times, with the officers up on the bridge!

I had another ego deflation. Upon being left alone at times as a bridge watchkeeper with the Chinese quartermaster, I felt that it was time for me to try chewing tobacco, as I did not like cigarettes and the Chief Officer appeared to enjoy his chew.

A short time after my experiment started, I found I did not like the taste. Having swallowed some of the juice I became sick over the side. When the captain on his lower bridge deck noticed me being sick over the side, he came to the bridge and told me not only to clean up my sickness but also the tobacco stains off the white paintwork where my spittle had sprayed during my chewing spree. So much for that experiment!

Chief Officer Atkinson and Jim McDonnell both spent a lot of time with me, and McDonnell was particularly patient as, being what one would call a school drop-out, I was pretty weak in algebra, geometry and the very important trigonometry so essential in celestial navigation. At that time I thought trigonometry was a part of the ship of which I had not heard! However, I persevered and I gradually mastered these subjects as well as learning to take a satisfactory noon sight.

When we reached Shanghai, I quickly made a beeline for the Harrop's and enjoyed their enormous hospitality once again. I took Girlie down to see the ship and for the first and only time was invited into the deck officer's saloon where those on board made Girlie and myself very welcome. We were given coffee, fancy cake and soft drinks, and both she and I enjoyed the visit. We were due to sail quite soon, so I had to decline an invitation to go to Woosung with the Harrop family and said my goodbyes for what proved to be the last time, although I did not know it then.

The young radio officer and myself knew we had a few hours left that last evening so we made our way ashore to the Navy YMCA. As so often happens a fight broke out and the Military Police were called. As soon as the fracas became obvious we made a dash for the washrooms and managed to climb through a window and shinny down a drain pipe to make our escape back to the ship. Our white uniforms were pretty dirty causing the captain to glare at us as we came aboard, but he made no comment. So far as we were concerned, we were just glad to be back without having been detained by the Military Police.

One memory comes to mind about an unusual duty which fell to me as a cadet. The officers liked to smuggle their girl friends on board which was against the rules. They had me act as lookout in case the captain was spotted returning to the ship. Of course wearing white, and perhaps acting a little agitatedly, I did not fool the captain. As soon as he was spotted I would tear down to the officers' cabins, warning them of the captain's approach. Overside went the girls and into a waiting sampan and that was that, or at least so I thought. Back in the fifties my wife and I were watching a soccer match at Ambleside in West Vancouver when I spotted a familiar face. It was an old and retired Captain Buchanan. We strolled over to say "hello" to the old gentleman, and after reintroducing myself I introduced him to my wife Eunice. He chuckled and said that I was the one who kept watch for the officers to warn them of his return to the ship, so they could get their girl friends off!

I guess school boys think that their masters know nothing of what they think they are discovering for the first time, and I suppose it seldom occurs to junior officers that the captain was a junior once himself, and no doubt knew all the tricks before some of us were even born!

After Shanghai we made for the usual range of Chinese ports, this time including Taku Bar, which is the port for the large inland city of Tientsin and is the closest Chinese port to Peking. After a call at Dairen where we loaded soya bean oil and peanuts again, we made for the Japanese port of Muroran on the island of Hokkaido, where we bunkered and took on a full general cargo for Vancouver.

The CITY OF VANCOUVER once again lived up to its reputation as an attracter of bad weather and this time it turned out to be another ordeal. We were burying ourselves in heavy seas at reduced speed, the aftermath of yet another typhoon, when a huge sea engulfed us on the starboard forward quarter, rolling aft. Due to a heavy starboard roll of the ship at that time, this massive wave engulfed the bridge wing where the chief officer was standing and snatched him overboard.

Life rings were thrown overboard, the ship slowed right down but no sign of the officer or the life rings could be seen. While still practically hove to looking for the mate, it was found that the anchor chain locker hatch was stove in. The second mate instructed me to take the bosun and three seamen forward to secure this hatch, as we were taking water down below. I was told by the master that he would blow a warning blast on the siren if he saw a wave approaching that looked as though it would inundate us.

Sure enough the warning blast was sounded just as we were driving wedges into the irons to batten down the hatch. I shouted to everyone to hang on as the ship plunged, burying the anchors in white spume, flooding the hawse pipes and then cascading all over the foredeck. There were outside guard rails, but nothing between us and the edge of the foredeck where it took a 16-foot drop into the well deck. The bosun and I were thrown into the starboard bulwarks, he escaping serious injury, but I received a broken arm and dislocated shoulder with head injuries. One seaman was killed outright when he and another ended up on the winches, the second man being injured but not fatally. The third man was lucky and was the least affected of us all.

We lost a seaman but regained our chief officer. While we were working forward on the stoved-in hatch, apparently the same sea that washed him off the bridge carried him back onto the aft well deck, where he was found by another Chinese crewman and brought back to his quarters. A miraculous survival, and fortunately without serious injury.

We reached Vancouver, and I was sent on sick leave after a medical examination which proved to be the end of my service in the CITY OF VANCOUVER and for Coughlin's. The CITY OF VICTORIA had recently been wrecked in Hakodate Strait, it is said after range lights had been tampered with by wreckers. With the VICTORIA, lost this left the company with just the one ship the VANCOUVER, which they promptly sold to V.K. Song, a Chinese owner based in Tsingtao. Song renamed her VEN-KOH and eventually she passed to Skibs A/S Thule managed by T.B. Torgersen of Oslo as the VENKOH. So far as can be determined, she lasted until 1948 when she evidently went to Far East shipbreakers.

For the time being at least this ended my service in deepsea tramps, and when I had sufficiently recovered from my injuries, I started to look for employment in the B.C. towboat industry.

Chapter Four

Home to British Columbia Coastal Service

After taking my sick leave from the CITY OF VANCOUVER, it was a little bit of a jolt when I learned that the John Coughlin Line had come to an end, as it turned out just a few short years before the second World War commenced. I have no doubt that had they continued in business, all of us who served in their ships would have been in heavy demand to man wartime deep sea shipping.

This was not to be in my own case as my injuries precluded any immediate return to deepsea ships, and quite apart from that there were simply no vacancies aboard any of the visiting foreign ships where my experience would have been handy.

After a short time I managed to get a job as cook-deckhand aboard the west coast steam-tug JWP. Her name was made up of the initials of John William Pike who originally built her. She was now owned by the MacFarlane Brothers. Captain George MacFarlane was master, and his brother Art MacFarlane was chief engineer.

They hired me as cook-deckhand. The cook part of my duties did not interest me very much, and in any event I was not a very good cook to start with. I could tell, that just as I was not impressed with my culinary achievements, no one else was either. What with hard and broken eggs, burned bacon and toast, underdone or overdone meats, it turned out that my best effort was boiled potatoes. In any event, matters came to a head the evening I decided to make sago pudding and I did it all wrong. The skipper was the first one to try it, and when he put his fork or spoon into it the whole lot came away like a block of rubber. His verdict was that I was not a cook and likely never would be, but he must have thought I was a pretty good deckhand, and decided to replace me as cook with a trained cook, while I would continue as deckhand. This was far better for all concerned, and gave us two full time deckhands.

We were towing bundle booms out of Port Renfrew for a big logging outfit called Cathol & Sorensen. After assembly at Port Renfrew, these would be towed in the open Pacific as Port Renfrew was outside the mouth of the Straits of Juan de Fuca, to Beecher Bay near Esquimalt. At Beecher Bay the bundle booms would be broken up and reassembled as flat rafts which we would tow into Puget Sound or to Vancouver and the Fraser River depending on who had purchased the logs. For the return trip we would sometimes tow a scow with logging equipment aboard for their logging show, and bring it back when empty to Victoria. The JWP was about 90 feet in length, and burned oil fuel, which was a lot cleaner and more convenient than coal. The master occupied a cabin behind the wheelhouse while the rest of the crew occupied the main accomodation below, in which was also located the galley and crew messroom. We two deckhands were the exception, in that we had a small fo'c'sle compartment under the foredeck with which I was quite happy.

I kept watch with the master while the other deckhand shared the mate's watch. This gave each of us a twelve hour day at the princely wage of $1 per day with all

Steam tug JWP
The subject of the amusing incident involving the hotel at Port Renfrew.

Diesel Fishing vessel ISPACO No. 2
Taken on charter by Captain George MacFarlane. The author was mate aboard this ship and recalls the "barking dog" navigation aid!

food found, but so far as bedding and such was concerned, everyone had to provide their own. Altogether I stayed with the JWP for eleven months until the parting of the ways came between the two brothers. George MacFarlane decided to go out on his own and chartered a small diesel tug, ex-fish packer called the ISPACO No. 2, and asked me to go along with him as his mate. The crew consisted of the master, myself as mate, a cook-deckhand and the engineer. I had started in the JWP as deckhand in 1934 and with ISPACO No. 2 in 1935 as mate. At this point I was 17, so realised that given my youth I was coming along quite well with my first appointment as mate.

The ISPACO No. 2 was about 60 feet in length, with a 65 hp heavy duty diesel, and while she did not have the towing capacity of the JWP, she was a lot more handy in that she could get right up to the camps herself, and tow her own bundles down the Jordan River to Port Renfrew, while the bigger tug had to wait around until some smaller boat brought the bundles out. It was an arrangement that the logging company liked because it tended to be more economical from their point of view. On the other hand, our smaller size and lower horsepower meant that we could not handle as big a boom as the JWP and this particularly showed up when bucking against heavy tides.

I remember coming on watch when the vessel and tow were abreast of Sheringham Point in the Straits of Juan de Fuca. Then the tide changed and we moved backwards so that if we were lucky we might have advanced by about four miles during the entire six hour watch, which meant a net speed over the ground of about 2/3rds of a knot, which felt like the speed of a tortoise.

Towing logs was not for the impatient in any event as the best speed one could normally expect over the ground would be perhaps 1.5 knots, and often less. Always of course we watched the weather like a hawk and prayed that a sudden turn would not find us in a badly exposed position, which might imperil our log tow just as it could endanger the tug. Believe me, the weather could be almost as bad and unpredictable in inside waters, such as off the Sunshine Coast, as it could be out in the Pacific. There were some compensations, one of which is widely used probably on all log towers, and that is to stream fishing lines overside as towing speed was also a good trolling speed. Some nice freshly caught fish on board always helped the cook's job, and surplus found its way home at the end of a trip.

I learned the need to keep a strict log, recording everything that was relevent such as bearings of lights and the time noted, weather wind and tide conditions and anything else pertinent to the safe handling of the tug and the tow, as without radar or depth-sounders or other modern aids, such as the ever present radio-telephone which we now take for granted, we were more or less flying by the seat of our pants.

Another instance which comes to mind was the occasion when we left Victoria for Cowichan Bay to pick up a tow of logs. I came on watch and took over from the skipper while we were going through Trial Island Pass heading for Coal Island Pass, near Schwartz Bay. Off Sidney, the engine started to slow down for no apparent reason, and eventually came to a stop, so I went down to the engine room to see what the problem was. There was a problem, and it was being created by the engineer who was messing around in the engine room, cussing about who had started his engine up. We were in fog and it was obvious that he was drunk, and I did not have time to argue with him so pushed him into his cabin and locked the door. I knew how to start the engine up, and we were soon under way again.

By now we were proceeding with caution as we were in thick fog and approaching Coal Island Pass. The skipper was not due on watch for a short while but I called him, given our position. I told him where we were and then recounted what had happened in the engine room. He asked me where the engineer was now, so I told him that he was still locked up. The skipper agreed that this was for the best, and was quite happy to leave him there to sober up. We entered the pass which was very narrow, and he put me up in the bow while he bounced echoes off the shore and asked me to count the seconds while they bounced back. Then he said "I'm going to give several short blasts on the whistle, so listen carefully and let me know if you hear anything". I told him I could hear nothing, except for the barking of a big dog.

"Oh that's fine" he said, "that's what I was hoping to hear, so I know exactly where we are. That's Mrs. Jones' dog and he always barks when he hears the short blasts on the whistle"!

When we got to Cowichan Bay and were relaxing over a cup of coffee before getting our tow under way, I said to George, "You know George, you've got me puzzled over navigating with the help of dogs and such. What would have happened if the dog had been at the vet's or had died the day before?" George MacFarlane looked at me and chuckled."Well, I would have been in trouble, would'nt I?"

This reminded me of another humorous incident in the JWP when we were tied up by Scott and Peden's grain wharf in Victoria harbour. The small grain boats, which were wooden steam freighters, used to come in there and one day one of them came surging up to the dock to make her landing. We could hear the bells and jingles from her engine room telegraph a long way off. George MacFarlane remarked that the skipper sure liked to play around with all her noise-makers. She might have been going too fast and looked like she was going to make a horrible landing. After many bells and jingles, lines were finally ashore and she was made fast, however we noticed that she was still surging ahead and then moving astern again. Just at that time her engineer came out on deck from the forward part of the engine room, so her master, seeing him, pulled his wheelhouse window down and said,

"I rang finished with engines. Don't you know what the bells and jingles mean?" The engineer took the pipe out of his mouth and spat overside.

"When I catch up to you I will be able to stop her. I'm so far behind on all your goddamned bells and jingles, I've still got a few moves to do". Bang went the wheelhouse window and that was the end of that conversation.

I guess this little scene illustrates the age old feud which went on in the old steamers between the master on the bridge and the engineer down below. In an emergency or a tight spot the man on the bridge cannot get action fast enough, while the very nature of operating a steam engine did not permit a response any faster than the engineer and his equipment's ability to react. Nowadays with modern diesels and bridge control of the engines, responses are a lot faster, being controlled by one man, but even so, a "full ahead" to emergency "full astern" can still not be

Steam Tug MCM
"She was a mess when we recommissioned her" at Victoria.

With the band of the 5th B.C. Coast Brigade Artillery in 1936.
The author seated third from right.

instantaneous as the engine has to have time to stop all its moving parts and go into the opposite cycle.

One story leads to another and reminds me of the time we were laying at Port Renfrew when I was still a deckhand in the JWP, waiting for logs. It was a Sunday and the B.C. Provincial Police were enforcing new liquor laws which closed the pubs on Sundays. This was quite a blow to tow boat men who usually enjoyed a few beers while they were killing time. The first time we were in there after the new laws came into being, the chief engineer and others made their way up to the pub located at the head of the dock and became pretty annoyed when they were told that the pub was not going to open any more on Sundays. They had had some booze on the boat so were already somewhat tanked up.

The next I knew was when I was ordered by the mate to take a line and pennant up to the hotel which I was to place right around the building and secure to our main tow line. The attitude was that if the hotel was not going to open on Sundays, we might as well get rid of it, by towing it away as it was no use anyway. Just then the police came down and put a stop to the whole farcical proceeding, but I am sure that if it had happened, the weight of our boat plus solid horsepower would have done quite a lot of damage. I have chuckled about this memory more than once, and it seems like it could make an excellent plot for some writer to build into a televison situation comedy!

The police were quite rough on the crew and made it very obvious that if there was any further nonsense they could all end up in jail. They passed me over as they could see how young I was, and that I had not been drinking. Quite apart from that, I was merely following orders. Captain McFarlane who was off watch and sleeping, was not aware of what had gone on until wakened by the police. Needless to say, the crew consisting of the mate, the chief and assistant engineer and cook were really told off. I was pretty scared, but he only had a fatherly talk with me which I took to heart.

Forty years later, when I was port captain with Seaspan, my assistant, Captain Jim Palmer and I were reminiscing one day about events from the past. The subject of the Port Renfrew Hotel and the incident of the JWP nearly towing it away came up. We both had a good laugh over that one,

"You were there at that time then"

"Indeed I was" I replied, "I was the one who was caught in the act of placing the line and pennant around the building when the police arrived on the scene".

"You know I heard all about that years later from my grandparents" he said, "they were the owners of the hotel!" Once again quite a small world.

In June 1936, Captain McFarlane decided to retire from towing and return the ISPACO NO. 2, to her owners. This put me out of a job at a time when there was nothing else available, so I went to work for my Dad at Crystal Springs Sodawater Company, driving a delivery truck around Victoria, but all the time keeping my eyes and ears open for another seagoing appointment. After some seven months of delivering sodawater, I got a phone call from George MacFarlane giving me the name and number of a Mr. Harry Kirby, who owned a taxi, and and had recently acquired a tugboat.

Mr. Kirby said that Captain MacFarlane had given me a very strong recommendation and that I knew the West Coast. I was hired as mate aboard his ancient coal burning steam tug, the MCM, in command of Captain Ernie Eastwood. The MCM had been unemployed for some time and was not in very good condition, so with a new master, myself as mate, a chief and assistant engineer, two deckhands and a cook, we turned to with a will to get her in shape for west coast of Vancouver Island towing. The two deckhands occupied bunks in the small fo'c'sle, while the rest of us were quartered on the main accomodation deck below the wheelhouse.

The chief engineer occupied a cabin on the starboard side while I had the equivalent on the port side and from then on it became a contest between us both. The ship was alive with cockroaches so when he came into his cabin he would spray them as they sat there on the bulkhead watching him. This act would drive them through the chinks in the planked bulkhead through to my side. When I came into my cabin I would go through the same process, and drive them through to him, but gradually we eliminated them, as well as the army of bed-bugs which infested the vessel.

Whenever we went into Union Bay to coal, we always ended up by piling it on deck as high as the bulwarks, as the bunkers were too small to hold sufficient fuel for a couple of round trips to the west coast. This meant that the deck was often awash until we had used enough to lighten ship, and what did not end up under the boiler sometimes was washed overboard as we made our way past Victoria to pick up our next tow.

I remember one trip when we were leaving the inner harbour to pick up a scow tied up in West Bay. The captain blew the customary three blasts on the whistle to warn the bridgeman at the Johnson Street bridge to open the bridge for us. Sure enough the railway section opened up immediately, but the road traffic part remained down. The MCM, being a steamer was fitted with the usual bell and jingle system for the bridge/engine-room telegraph. But before finishing this story, let me explain that the working of the telegraph may sound confusing to the layman, but really it was not, once you had learned the signals. Perhaps the following will explain the system for the uninitiated:-

Going from STOP -	1 gong meant half ahead
	A jingle before the gong meant slow ahead
	A jingle after the gong meant full ahead
	2 gongs meant half astern
	A jingle before two gongs meant slow astern
	A jingle after two gongs meant full astern
From Full AHEAD -	1 gong meant slow to half ahead
	2 gongs meant, stop
	A jingle after full ahead meant full away
	A jingle after stop meant, finished with engines
	A jingle after full away meant, standby.

A deckhand and myself were at the stern getting our gear ready for the scow we planned to pick up after clearing the bridge. The engine was stopped and we were just drifting ahead, waiting for the bridge to be fully opened. I heard one gong, and the engine moved into the half ahead position with a surge of water under the stern, but the bridge was still down and we were clearly going to hit it. I could see what was about to happen so I ran to the engine room and shouted to go full astern, but it was too late.

We hit the bridge with our foremast which snapped off, but fortunately the pilot house was low enough to escape. When the stack contacted the bridge it brought us to a stop, and while the funnel was not broken off, it was quite badly bent. This required us to go to the local shipyard to get it straightened and have a new mast fitted. In the post mortem that followed it was quickly found that the connecting lanyard from the bridge telegraph to the engine room had broken as the skipper gave her the second gong, thus meaning that the engineroom had only received the first gong. It was an act that followed upon the general deterioration in the vessel, so no one could be blamed for the accident.

Bob Frane was our chief engineer. He owned a little steam launch of his own, about 18 feet long. I thought she was a pretty unique little vessel as he ran around the harbour in her, burning whatever he could find in the way of scrap wood and bark. She used to run at quite a good speed, with smoke trailing out of her tall thin stack. You would have to agree that a man who spent his time at sea running a steam tug, and who then came ashore on his days off, and ran a little steam launch for his own fun, must have been quite a steamboat enthusiast!

I served in the MCM for ten months and then she was tied up, but fortunately the JWP came back on the run and I was able to move over to her under a new skipper, Captain MacPhee, with only one day off in between. The JWP ran on the Port Renfrew run for three months, and then she was replaced by a diesel tug called the FAIRBANKS. This meant that I was out of a job again so went back to delivery work for my Dad, until I found another ship. This new vessel was a Danish lumber carrier called the STJERNEBORG and was about the same size as my previous two deepsea ships, the DANWOOD and CITY OF VANCOUVER. It was good to have another opportunity of going deep sea again, but little did I know that this was to be my last deepwater ship.

Chapter Five

Another Deep-Sea Voyage

After spending three months back in the soda water business I was fortunate enough to locate a berth in the Danish Motor Vessel STJERNEBORG, a typical modern Scandinavian tramp of 4551 grt, built in 1929 by Burmeister & Wain at Copenhagen for A/S D/S Dannebrog, a company managed by the well-known Danish shipping firm of C.K. Hansen.

Another friend of mine, John Hamilton, signed on as officer's messboy, while I was taken on as quartermaster. We did our usual loading with B.C. lumber, starting at Cowichan Bay and thence up the Fraser to Fraser Mills, topping off in Vancouver. We sailed fully laden for New York with discharge at Erie Basin followed by unloading the remainder of our cargo at Irvington and Albany, N.Y.

As a seaman quartermaster, my job was different than aboard other ships in which I had previously served. I stood regular watches taking my turn as helmsman, but when in port had few duties so again did my watch on the gangway acting as security for the ship. One incident I remember when at the wheel steering the ship up to Irvington was a conversation between the master and the pilot. In view of the prevailing wind condition the master was concerned about berthing the ship, but was assured by the pilot that there would be no problem. Because there was a tide running, we had to go past Irvington, turn and come back downriver to the berth. We came in and made a pretty fair landing, even though we had quite a lot of way on. The dock men got our spring line on to the shore side bollard but somehow it must have been fouled on our deck and broke.

Now when a wire line breaks it becomes an extremely lethal weapon and can do a great deal of damage as it reacts to the released strain like a whipping snake, particularly if anyone gets in its way. I heard our captain say "Oh, my God" as he quickly saw that one man had been killed instantly, as the line practically cut his torso in two, and a second man badly injured. Berthing had been against the captain's better judgement, and then I saw something I had never seen before and have not seen since. He ordered the pilot off the bridge and took the vessel out in the stream and anchored.

While we were in Erie Basin, John and I decided to go into Manhattan and do it right this time. I was wearing my old cadet uniform from CITY OF VANCOUVER days, minus the brass buttons and insignia, having turned it into an ordinary suit. I forget the name of the posh hotel we went to for their dinner dance, but I noticed a very pretty girl at the next table and eventually got up enough courage to ask her for a dance. In fact we had two dances and after exchanging pleasantries and who we were, and from where we came, it turned out that she was the Hollywood starlet Anita Louise, who was busy making a name for herself in the movies. As it turned out that was to be as close as I ever got to knowing anyone from the "culluloid capital of the world" as it is sometimes called!

Danish diesel freighter "STJERNEBORG"
The authors third and last deepsea ship

The STJERNEBORG was quite old fashioned in one regard for such a modern ship, in that she had an open bridge so far as the helmsman was concerned. The only shelter was the waist high solid bridge rail which formed the bulwark of the bridge about six feet ahead of the helmsman's position. The chartroom was about five feet behind where the helmsman stood, so if he were at the wheel, he either got scorched by the sun, saturated by the rain, or frozen by the wind or snow.

A few owners stayed with this out of date arrangement long after most modern ships had adopted enclosed bridges and wheelhouses, presumably on the theory that in the circumstances there was little likelihood of the helmsman falling asleep at the wheel! On the port and starboard wings of the bridge there were wing shelters which were what was commonly known as "dog houses", where the mate could stand his watch sheltered and in relative comfort. Why helmsmen should be signalled out for such inconsiderate treatment escapes me.

Coming back through the Panama Canal, the mosquitoes were very bad and about three of us who were infected including myself, could not get any quinine as the ship had run out of it, such was the demand on board. This affected me quite badly and for some years after I was married I would have problems as a result of my malaria returning. One effect of this was that I was never allowed to subsequently give blood to the Red Cross. We returned to B.C. where we recommenced loading lumber for New York. Following discharge we got a change of orders and went into Norfolk, Virginia to load scrap steel for Japan.

It was quite interesting to see the rail gondola cars, pushed by steam engines, moved into place alongside our ship where a huge electro-magnetic crane would plunge into the car and retrieve a mass of steel scrap then swing over our hold, cut off the power and the whole mass would fall into our hold with a tremendous clatter. I had never had any experience with ore cargoes but I am told that they and scrap steel are probably among the most destructive to a ship as the pounding taken by the bottom plates in a ship's hold can shorten the life of a vessel if done often enough. Of course it is particularly bad until sufficient material is aboard to act as a cushion.

In my day when going deep sea, the majority of such heavy and destructive cargoes were shipped in regular tramp vessels, not specifically designed for the job, and the result was sometimes improperly loaded cargoes resulting in very "stiff" ships, lacking in sea-kindly ability. The result has been that a number of major casualties have been caused by the nature of the cargo itself, rather than any lack of inherent quality of design and construction in the ship herself. Too frequently it was a case of mismatching the ship and the cargo. Nowadays of course, with the advent of the large bulk-carrier, such ships are built with special attention to strengthening for ore and heavy cargoes such as minerals and scrap. Even then, that is not a guarantee against structural failure in the hull contributed to by the nature of such heavy cargoes setting up stresses, and a number of modern ships have been lost, as a consequence.

From Norfolk we proceeded to San Pedro to take on bunkers for the long stretch over the Pacific where we were to go to the Yawata Steel Works to unload our cargo. I was most surprised as we approached the port of Moji to be met by a Japanese naval vessel which boarded our ship and put an armed guard on board with one man guarding the bridge and a second the engine-room. Our radio was also sealed and obviously the Japanese were very security conscious and on a war footing, as indeed was the case as the Sino-Japanese war had been under way since 1934. This was 1938, three years before Pearl Harbour, and it is interesting to reflect on the fact that Japan drew most of its oil from the U.S., either Texas or California, with Japanese tankers being regular visitors at San Pedro, for example. In fact the very U.S. originated scrap we were delivering was possibly destined to be fired back at the western powers, particularly the U.S., or go into new warships and tanks.

We tied up to bouys in Moji Harbour with some eight other freighters to await orders to proceed alongside the Yawata Steel Works. After laying at the bouys for about ten days, we went into the Yawata dock and joined two other freighters there. It was a pretty boring time as shore leave for any reason other than an emergency was forbidden and while alongside a guard was posted at the foot of the gangway. I got fed-up with this and decided to visit the ship ahead of us, so I went down a ladder hanging from the stern bulwarks which was insecurely tied. The ladder suddenly fell and threw me off, injuring both my ankles which when examined proved to have slight fractures in each. This required a short spell in hospital where the diet was chicken at every meal. I am sure the Japanese hospital people thought that this was all that white people ate, which only added to the boredom of being at Yawata.

After completing discharge, we left Yawata for a return trip to Norfolk for another cargo of scrap. Norfolk, is of course, one of the main bases for the U.S. Navy, in fact it is the headquarters of its Atlantic fleet. It conveyed a totally different atmosphere to any other port I had ever been in, with a vast array of all types of warships including one which I remember, the aircraft carrier SARATOGA, which was to make a name for herself in the Pacific war still to come.

The return to Japan was a repeat of the first trip, but this time we lay at the bouys for far longer. However, we were permitted to go ashore in the town of Moji for a welcome shore leave. One diversion we suffered was a machine-gun strafing by aircraft which turned out to be Chinese. We suffered no casualties and no significant damage, although how the other ships fared is not known to me. Eventually we went alongside to discharge at Yawata Steel Works and again were confined to the ship with no shore leave.

We came back from Japan in ballast bound for B.C., this time very frequently in thick fog, and without modern navigation aids. We had to proceed by dead reckoning, for which purpose the log trailing astern was very important in giving us our daily mileage. However, one of the other quartermasters was a young German fellow who possesssed a pet monkey called "Willi" who enjoyed the run of the ship and was always getting into mischief. The duties of the quartermaster were to read the log and report the reading to the bridge, which could then calculate the speed of the ship over the ground and log the mileage. One day much confusion reigned aboard ship when it was discovered that the log was giving an incorrect reading, in fact the ship was going backwards according to it. They could not figure out what had happened and the master was pretty concerned, particularly when a few days later the log indicated that the ship had been travelling "at 50 knots", which was very good for a ship never normally capable of more than 11 knots!

The cause of the trouble was noticed by someone who happened to look at the log at the right time. There was Willi the monkey, being a monkey and interfering with the log. He had seen his master and perhaps others like me tending the log, and had gone out on the arm from which it hung to play with it. After this Willi was confined to quarters where he got into further mischief, being found one day in another crewman's cabin. He got into the man's supply of cigarettes and stripped the paper off them all to spread the tobacco around the cabin. Monkeys are well known for their mischievousness, and Willi did not let his tribe down in any way when it came to this sort of activity.

As we approached the B.C. coast, we managed to obtain a few sun sights so that the bridge could correctly check our position. In spite of being in fog over almost the entire length of the voyage across the Pacific, we made a perfect landfall as we entered the Straits of Juan de Fuca, picked up our pilot off Victoria and arrived in Vancouver. This was the appropriate time for me to sign off as I was not too well following the sickness caused by malaria and the damage to my ankles. I did not know it at the time, but after the STJERNEBORG left Vancouver for Cowichan Bay, she was joined there by another old friend of mine, Norman Heaslip, who signed on as messman and did about six months in the vessel. I heard by phone from Norman over the years but never actually saw him until very recently, when he turned up at my home near Sechelt, and we had the opportunity of seeing each other for the first time in 52 years!

I said goodbye to the STJERNEBORG with some regret, not knowing that this now terminated my association with foreign-going deep-sea ships. The STJERNEBORG was a typical, well run Scandinavian ship, clean, efficient and always well maintained and manned by a good group of officers and crew.

My father had now retired from the Crystal Springs Soda Water Company, and he and my mother were living at Vesuvius Bay on Saltspring Island. My brother and a friend were running the soda water business in Victoria, but Dad had it up for sale. I spent Christmas and New Year with them, and, while there, went to a dance at the golf club with some of my old high school friends. I spotted a young girl there who was standing perhaps somewhat shyly by herself and asked a friend, "who is she?".

"Don't bother with her" he replied, "she is just a high school kid!"

I persisted and went over to her and introduced myself. We spent most of the evening together, and I escorted her home. That is how I met Eunice Roberts, who became my wife in 1940!

Chapter Six

Coastal Ships Again

In late March of 1939, just past my twenty-first birthday, I was pleased to receive a call to say that I had been recommended by someone I do not now recall, for a job on the tug NAHMINT of which Captain Shaddy was master. This was a nice break after filling in on a shore job since coming ashore from the STJERNEBORG. I was hired following a brief interview and joined my new boat which was some 90 feet in length, with a 100hp Fairbanks Morse diesel which had to be warmed with a punk before the air start. In addition to the master and myself as mate, there was a chief engineer who assisted on deck also when needed. The fourth crew member was a cook-deckhand and with no extra deckhand, I stood my watches alone.

NAHMINT was employed in towing bundle booms out of Nitinat Lake, north of Port Renfrew. The lake was a new experience for me, involving coming in from the open Pacific and crossing the shallow bar into the lake, with a rock bound coast to the north and the south. Entering involved fine judgement as it was necessary to roll in on the incoming swells and then execute a sharp turn to port, and a move at the wrong time could result in going up on the beach with loss of life as had happened with less fortunate boats in the past.

One personal accident I experienced had its moments of humour. This occured in Port Angeles when we were loading bundle wires on to the tug in the darkness. I misjudged the fact that the tug had moved slightly from the boom float and I put my foot where I thought I was stepping on to the tug's rubbing strake. There was nothing there, so I took an unwelcome fall into the water with the wires over my shoulder which naturally carried me down like a stone. I managed to drop them off under water and came up where the deckhand reached me with a boat hook. Captain Shaddy said that I was not supposed to fall in the water with company property, unless I brought it back with me, as it all cost money! On the other hand, I always figured that if one fell in the water with heavy seaboots on, it was smart to check his direction as he was going under so that when he did reach bottom, he could then "run like hell" for the shallowest water!!

An incident which finished my days on the NAHMINT involved a towing winch accident. In June 1939, we were bringing in our line when it fouled, and while heaving on it to free it, my gloved left hand was caught under the wire and I was dragged onto the winch. Fortunately the chief engineer came on deck at that moment and saw what had happened. He stopped the winch immediately. Just the same my injuries consisting of a dislocated left shoulder, and badly wrenched back were serious enough to keep me ashore for eleven months. It was bad enough that it happened at all, but I was glad that as it did occur, it took place in Victoria, near a decent hospital rather than at some remote place out on the west coast.

While recuperating I took a turn at selling cars for Len Jones, a Victoria car dealer who had the agency for the Morris Oxford. However, due to my previous injuries I went into hospital in August for several months. Upon arriving back on

Saltspring Island from hospital, on New Year's Day 1940, I met Eunice for the second time, and we started going out together regularly as steady friends, which continued until July when we got married. In the spring of 1940, my father and I got together and bought a small fishboat-packer type of vessel called the MARION which we planned to employ around the Gulf Islands. I sailed her down from Saltspring to Sidney to put her on the ways for bottom cleaning and painting, and was not too happy with the way she handled coming around Beaver Point, Saltspring Island, in a south easterly slop. I was even less happy making our landing at Sidney, because when I put her in reverse the propeller came off! I talked it over with Dad, and we decided she was not quite what we wanted so we put her up for sale and fortunately sold her quite quickly.

We had heard of a little packer-freighter which was working around the Gulf Islands and was also for sale. This vessel called the THL, was named after Thomas Hudson Lee and became known to us as the "Top Heavy and Leaky". She was operating a freight service among the islands which we continued after we purchased her with the aid of some bank finance. She was a handy vessel with a length of 57 feet and was powered by a 100 hp Stirling gas engine, which was something of an unusual combination in that after starting on gas and reaching the required engine temperature it could then be switched to diesel fuel. She had a raised forecastle with a larger hold forward and smaller hold aft, with the engine room and accomodation between.

We used to go into Schwartz Bay long before there was any thought of that place being a major ferry terminal, to load Buckerfields' animal feeds and hay for distribution among the Gulf Islands. The war of course was now underway and the Army contacted us. They wanted to charter the THL for servicing their needs around Prince Rupert, and they hired me as a civilian skipper employed on their ships because they did not have qualified military personnel of their own. My first job after the charter was initiated, was to deliver the THL to the Canadian Army Service Corps in Prince Rupert. Aside from the brief period while I operated the THL for our own account, this was my first appointment as master which I had achieved by the time I was 22.

Before going into Army service, Eunice used to come down to the boat to make pies and similar goodies for us which were greatly appreciated by the crew and myself. Eunice's younger brother, Harry Roberts, was then about fifteen years old and used to work as deckhand on the boat when not in school. Eunice had just taken two pies out of the oven and had placed one on the table and the other on the bench to cool. Just then Harry came into the cabin and saw the pies, picking up the one which was on the table, and promptly dropped it on the deck. In his excitement and embarrassment, he then sat down and managed to sit on the other pie. Needless to say, Harry was not the most popular person on board that day!

Another story involving my brother-in-law might have had more tragic consequences even though it took nothing away from his youthful exuberance in seeking to do a good job aboard ship. We were coming up through Trial Island Pass when the gas engine started to act up. Water in the fuel line seemed the obvious answer and, as it was blowing up a bit, I decided to anchor while we sorted the problem out. I sent Harry up to the forecastle to drop the anchor, but unfortunately he neglected to check that the anchor chain was not attached, so suddenly we were

A sunny day with the Army in Prince Rupert.

minus our only anchor. Fortunately the engineer managed to bleed the fuel line in sufficient time to keep us away from the nearby rocks. I was concerned about Eunice who happened to be aboard, so I had her rowed ashore in the dinghy where she visited a nearby house to use their phone to call for assistance, which arrived in due course and towed us in.

On the way up to Prince Rupert, we got into a bad blow in Johnstone Straits near Kelsey Bay, an area of the coast with which I had no familiarity at that time. The crew were all up on deck, so I asked the deckhand to go below to see how things were as the boat was feeling sluggish. He went into the forecastle and stepped into water which confirmed that we had a fair-sized leak. We started the pumps and managed to make Alert Bay where we had her put on the ways. An examination showed that she had opened up on both sides of the keel forward. However, the yard was able to fix the problem and we went on our way bound for Prince Rupert. Crossing Queen Charlotte Sound in this very small ship proved to be no picnic but once across, the rest of the trip to Prince Rupert was uneventful except for fog.

We were assigned a berth at the RCASC dock along with other vessels in army service. My civilian crew who had brought the boat up from Victoria returned home, while I was assigned army personnel as crew. The army supplied me with a mate, engineer and deckhand. I found out that my job was to deliver supplies to outlying posts, along with personnel and the odd concert party at night, as well as occasionally patrolling outside the harbour, and doing anything else that was required from a marine point of view. The three fortifications which we served in the immediate area were Fort Barrett and Fort Frederick, which were equipped with heavy guns, one each side of the entrance to Prince Rupert Harbour, and Fort Dundas, a machine gun post on Metlakatla Channel.

We were on 24 hour standby duty. Our day commenced with carrying supplies and civilian workers out to the forts in the morning, as they were still under construction, and bringing back anything that needed returning to Prince Rupert. In the late afternoon we would bring the workers home and might go out again in the evening to deliver a YMCA concert party to the forts, standing by to redeliver them to Prince Rupert after it was all over. In the forward hold, we carried everything that was required by the outpost including all stores and ammunition.

Eunice and I had announced our engagement before I left to bring the THL up to Prince Rupert, but as I had now been able to find an apartment there, which was not easy in wartime, it was agreed that she would leave Vancouver on the Monday, and we would be married by the Army Service Corps padre on the Thursday. However, I got a call on the Friday prior, to report to Vancouver for a medical for the R.C.N.V.R. so that I arrived in Vancouver a little before she was due to leave for Prince Rupert. As matters turned out, we were able to marry on the Tuesday, July 16, 1940 on Saltspring Island, which gave a good opportunity to have our families there, which would have been out of the question in Prince Rupert.

I had my navy medical in Victoria on the 18th and was turned down for medical reasons. I also tried to join the Army and Air Force Marine Divisions Corps but the results were the same, so that was it so far as any of the services were concerned, and I was given a discharge as being unfit for any further call for duty. Colonel Roome, commanding officer of the R.C.A.S.C. detachment at Prince Rupert heard of this and said he would like me to go back up there to continue running Army vessels, so my new bride and I caught the C.P.R. steamer PRINCESS ALICE. Life in Prince Rupert was quite hectic during the war, and the place suffered from a lot of overcrowding with Canadian and American service people.

There was an important seaplane base at Seal Cove and the Prince Rupert Shipyard was busy with war work and would later go on to build 10,000 ton freighters. We managed to find a larger apartment with two bedrooms, but were promptly told that we would have to take in a roomer which was not what we had in mind. That was fair enough though considering the great shortage of accomodation, and we took in a shipyard worker who turned out to be a very nice fellow.

We had one serious accident with the THL before Eunice came up. On this occasion we were taking troops up to one of the forts as well as ammunition, when there was a sudden explosion in the engine room. The gas engine had an explosion and breached a fuel line, so that within seconds there was a raging fire below. We got the troops off and fortunately we were in the city so the fire department came down and saved the vessel. The engine room was damaged quite severely, but fortunately the engine room bulkhead held and kept the fire from getting into the hold and igniting the explosives on board. The gas engine was a write-off and Dad replaced it with a Buda diesel, which was a big improvement in terms of efficiency and safety.

It was really something to be a civilian skipper with an army crew. Most had no experience at all, so they had to be trained as we went along. Some of them ended up on the boats after having committed some misdemeanor ashore. One fellow I had aboard had been the colonel's driver and on an occasion of some importance had driven the colonel to the function with instructions to wait. Whatever it was, our fellow had decided to go off with the car and go spooning with his girl friend. They must have both gone off to sleep until the military police found him and the car. This cost him his job and resulted in him getting his berth on my boat, the THL.

On another occasion we had an army officer join our crew temporarily as mate, and that was quite an experience. He questioned my judgement on everything, including the weather and the capabilities of the boat. He was the type who knew it all, as one day we were at anchor off Fort Frederick and he wanted to go ashore to deliver a payroll. It was pretty rough on the beach and I suggested he wait awhile until the sea had calmed down. He would have none of it and insisted on being rowed ashore. We asked him to sit in the middle of the boat, but again he was having none of that and sat in the stern. When the boat reached the beach and the oarsman got out, the next wave filled the boat so that one very wet army officer resulted. When he got back, he accused the deckhand of deliberately swamping the boat, which might have been true, as the officer was just sufficiently obnoxious that it would be a temptation for someone to do a trick like that!

Another time we got a call at night to take two officers out to Fort Dundas in the Metlakatla Channel. This time I had a different boat called the SYLENE and was short handed with just an engineer and a deckhand on board. They were impatient to get out even though I told them that I would prefer to leave it for another two or three hours as there was a very strong tide running at this time. They were very impatient and insisted that they wanted to go without further delay, and as I anticipated, when we arrived there was a strong tide running with the water too low to be able to come alongside the dock. We were in the process of dropping anchor and they fussed and fumed about getting ashore right away. I told them that that would follow once I was sure that the anchor was holding and we were safely anchored. While we were busy up on the foredeck, we heard shouts and saw them both in the water. They had taken it upon themselves to launch the ship's boat and row themselves ashore, but had not noticed that the bung was not inserted in the bottom of the boat. As soon as the boat hit the water, with their additional weight, she sank quickly and we fished them out with boat hooks. With the weight of their greatcoats, the fast tide, and the darkness, they had seconds before being lost from sight followed by almost certain drowning.

Another episode worth mentioning was the occasion when we were doing duty as examination vessel outside Prince Rupert. A fairly large fishing vessel approached, but did not stop as she passed us, so we contacted the port and told them of this. They fired a shot across her bows but she took no notice. A second shot was fired, and this time the fisherman in the wheel house came out on deck to see what the splash was, when a third shot landed nearby. This time he got the message and hurriedly reversed. When we caught up with her we found that there was only this very old fisherman on board who did not really understand that there was a war on, and this was part of the security arrangements for the port.

On another occasion the port told us that there were three unidentified vessels off to the west proceeding northwards and that we should investigate. They ignored our signal, so while we were busy getting our armament of .303 rifles ready, a belated reply came through to the effect that they were U.S. Navy vessels bound for Alaska. What a good job we did not fire, for they had the firepower to blow us out of the water!

I was advised by Colonel Roome that the first of their new boats would be delivered shortly and that our contract with the THL would be terminated at the end of the year, but in the meantime I was asked to bring the first vessel up from Victoria for the Army. We gave up our apartment in Prince Rupert and Eunice came down with me to stay with my parents at Saltspring Island. The first of these new army boats was the GENERAL CALDWELL. This was followed by the GENERAL LAKE and GENERAL ANDERSON, all three of which I delivered.

With this, the THL's charter came to an end and I returned the vessel to the Gulf Islands, using her as before in general freighting.In the meantime my parents had purchased a summer hotel called Vesuvius Lodge, and after a family meeting, we decided to sell the THL and buy a smaller cruiser type vessel which could be used in conjunction with the lodge for charters and outings for lodge guests, as well as using her as a passenger vessel carrying up to eight passengers, between Vesuvius Bay and Crofton, before there was any ferry. Eunice and I helped Mum and Dad run the lodge and also looked after the boat. Another duty to which I attended was picking up lodge guests by car from the C.P.R. PRINCESS MARY. It was while we were at the lodge that our eldest son Dan was born in 1941 and Eunice became busy as a Mum.

I must say that the lodge was very busy and successful during this period. It was always full, and bookings were made well ahead, as people from a wide area came to enjoy a little quiet respite from the stresses of war. Admittedly we were little affected by the carnage of war in British Columbia, but the economy was more and more shifting over to a war footing, with lots of our young men and women joining up and finding themselves in places they never dreamed they would ever see. Pearl Harbour occurred on December 7, 1941, so the possibilities of the war spreading to our side of the Pacific became much more of a reality.

The lodge had a beautiful dining room with a verandah which swept around the south west corner. Periodically we would get a radio call from the ferry CY PECK when she was on one of her cruises through the Gulf Islands, and all of a sudden we would end up with a hundred passengers for lunch. To say the least, such short notice arrivals created a lot of hectic activity, but we still managed to cope with them in a very satisfactory way.

I remember one small amusing incident concerning the PRINCESS MARY. We had a guest who was something of a comedian. He came down with me to see the ship come in. I explained to him how they moored the ship when she came alongside. A seaman would throw a heaving line ashore attached to the spring line,

Canadian National Railway's PRINCE RUPERT aboard which the author served as quartermaster. Shown in Grand Trunk Pacific colours.

which once placed over the shore-side bollard enabled the ship to walk her way into the berth. In my usual way of kidding people, I said that the ship paid fifty cents to the shore side man for taking the line and placing it over the bollard.When the PRINCESS MARY's heaving line was thrown ashore, the comedian grabbed it, doing exactly what I had explained, and then shouted up to the bridge that he wanted his fifty cents. The captain replied that, "We don't pay anyone for doing jobs like that". Our comedian immediately returned to the spring line which still had slack in it and threw it back in the water. This caused laughter on the dock and consternation on the ship which was alongside but momentarily out of control, until they got another line ashore. I thought to myself that I should keep my big mouth shut and not put these mischievous ideas into innocent heads!

After the summer of 1942 I was starting to get itchy feet about going back to sea, and was looking around for a suitable job. Harold Elworthy of Island Tug & Barge Ltd. had bought a tug called the ELDOMA and I was hired as mate, going over to join her at New Westminster to bring her over for general towing work out of Victoria. I spent seven months in her as mate, but was starting to have troubles with my back again, through handling the heavy gear. Island Tug put me down below as second engineer, looking after the big Union diesel which powered her, but this did not last, as I found I had a bad allergy to diesel oil fumes, so I had to take my leave of Island Tug and the ELDOMA.

With great determination, I decided that I must stay at sea, and never having served in passenger ships decided to contact Canadian National Steamships. The company operated a service up coast out of Vancouver to Prince Rupert and Alaskan ports with the three-stack passenger steamers PRINCE RUPERT and PRINCE

GEORGE. Because of wartime conditions, newer ships on the company's service had been transferred off the route for naval service, with the result that both ships were always loaded to capacity with passengers and freight, even to the extent that the forecastle was used as passenger accomodation being classified as "steerage". Other passengers used cots out on the open freight deck wherever sufficient shelter could be found.

Within a week I was hired as a lookout and shortly after promoted to quartermaster, which meant that once again I would take the wheel of a large ship. Normally we left Monday night at 9 pm, stopping at Ocean Falls, Prince Rupert, Ketchikan and Skagway, returning to Vancouver on Saturday.

This routine continued for several months, until the combined Canadian and U.S. Army Transport Corps, took the ships over for a new extended trip from Prince Rupert to Alaskan ports beyond our normal range. We arrived at Prince Rupert at the end of our regular upcoast trip, where the vessel was then reloaded for Alaska with military cargo and personnel, for what would be a two week trip. When we arrived back at Prince Rupert the PRINCE GEORGE would then go on the route and we would resume our regular trip to Vancouver and so on, the two ships alternating with each other in this new routine. We had a gun mounted on the stern manned by three R.C.N. ratings, and both ships were painted in wartime grey, as of course conditions demanded it and we were sailing into a war zone. Japanese forces were now lodged in certain of the American Aleutian Islands, which brought the war home to North Americans in a particular way, as this was the only point where the North American continent was invaded by the enemy.

I left the PRINCE RUPERT in 1943. It was an interesting experience, and a lot of credit has to be given to the masters and crews for keeping those ships going on a regular schedule without serious mishap, particularly taking into account that all coastal lights had been extinguished, and navigation to a large extent was by dead reckoning and "the seat of one's pants". Without aids such as shore lights and before we had radar, one can imagine the hazards of maintaining a regular schedule in fog, blizzards and heavy rainstorms.

I only recall one bad incident when we were approaching Cape Mudge just south of Campbell River. We bucked into a strong south easterly, with a heavy swell which worked against the flood tide and threw up huge short waves. The master rang for half speed, then slow, and eventually brought her to a stop as huge seas cascaded over the forecastle, smashed into the bridge and ran like a runaway creek along the boat deck. Being out in the open was no place to be, and three cars tied down on the forward hatch were a total loss. It is no wonder that tugboat men regard Cape Mudge as one of the worst trouble spots on the B.C. coast!

Another very bad trouble spot which has taken quite a few lives and a number of vessels was Ripple Rock, placed by nature right in the middle of Seymour Narrows, north of Menzies Bay. When the tide was at its greatest strength with southbound floods and northbound ebbs, the tide going through there had ferocious strength. Add to this any weather condition working against the direction of the tide, and here again a vessel could experience short steep overwhelming seas. Going through the Seymours, as they were called, required precise timing, and consummate skill on the part of masters to minimise danger to the ship and the people on board. Now that the rock has been removed, the worst danger has gone with it, so that large bulk carriers and oversize tows such as fully laden log barges negotiate it every day. But it still requires respect.

We had a bad experience with Ripple Rock due to being delayed in leaving Vancouver for Prince Rupert, so that when we did get into the narrows we were bucking a powerful flood tide. The engines were turning out maximum power and the ship was vibrating under the effort. We came up to Maude Island before we made the turn into the worst of the tide, but after inching forward we were eventually held by the force of the current. After about fifteen minutes of trying, the captain did the only thing he could and slowly eased her back to a point where we could turn the vessel and run into Menzies Bay to lay at anchor for about three hours until the worst was over.

Funny instances abounded when dealing with humanity on a passenger vessel, including new green crewmen. On one occasion I was on my way down below for a "mug-up" when a new crewman on the boat deck stopped me and asked me what those "things" were. He was referring to the ventilators of which we had quite a few of the big cowl type. I told him that they were fog catchers specially fitted to catch fog and store it in the fog locker down below. Being wartime still, the idea was to have this fog ready to release in the event we were chased by an enemy vessel, rather like a smoke screen. He nodded sagely and I parted company stating, "now you keep that to yourself as it really is a top secret matter, which should not be spread around". To the amusement of the crew the word spread like wildfire around the ship. The guy could simply not keep a secret!

We used to get quite a few ladies of easy virtue travelling aboard the ships and they were not slow in plying their wares for the benefit of anyone so inclined. One day one of these women approached me perhaps a little the worse for wear as the result of alcohol, and asked if she could see the captain. I asked her what for, and she replied with,

"Oh, he's such a nice man. I'd like to have a talk with him".

I decided this might be good for a laugh, so being a quarter master I always had access to the bridge which in turn gave access directly to the captain's cabin. I took her up with me and knocked discreetly on the captain's door. He cleared his throat and said "yes" as only a condescending captain can do.

"Excuse me, sir. There's a lady here who would like to speak to you" I said.

"Is it very important" he asked. "Well, she seems to think it is" I replied.

He was just getting dressed in his best uniform, to go down for dinner, so he opened the door, whereupon the lady threw her arms around him and gave him a big kiss saying,

"Oh dearie, I've been wanting to meet you for such a long time" she gushed.

No doubt the captain threw her off, but I did not stay around long enough to see the result. The third mate and duty quartermaster could hear what was going on and were splitting their sides, and from them the story quickly spread through the entire ship. The captain was a dignified type of man and the reader can imagine the dressing down I got from him at the first opportunity he had.

On another occasion, we had the relief captain in charge who was a totally different type, being "a hale fellow well met" sort who enjoyed a good joke. On this occasion we were both leaving the bridge, he to go to the officers' mess, and me to the petty officers' mess. As we walked along the companion way, we could see men standing in a line-up outside of a first class cabin. Not everyone was into this kind of thing, but we knew what these fellows had on their minds.

"Okay fellows break it up, we all like what you're planning on doing at times, but you need'nt make it so goddamn obvious. Break it up" said the captain as we pushed past them.

We used to load a lot of American liquor aboard while in Army Transport service out of Prince Rupert. It was being shipped by rail from the east. While in transit, many cases were damaged and broken open with much of the contents pilfered. Some of this became fair game for crew who broached the cases and helped themselves, and it was not just the unlicensed personnel who got their hands on it. It was nice to have one's own private supply, of course, but some of it was bootlegged to passengers returning from Alaska ports. We had to take care when the customs officers came aboard, as going into Alaska and returning to Canada meant that we were in international trade. We three quarter-masters shared quarters which meant that as we were also watchkeepers, one of us was always asleep. Whoever it was, we simply put whatever bottles we wished alongside the body of the "sleeping" man. The customs officers understood watchkeeping so never disturbed a sleeper, which was an arrangement which suited us fine!

Once, we were coming into Prince Rupert from our transport trip to Alaska under Captain Caldwell. As we came up the harbour, he could see that the berth he was to go to was too short for the ship, so he radioed that the wharfinger should shift a freighter down the dock to leave adequate room for the PRINCE RUPERT. Back came a sarcastic reply. "You Canadians, what do you need the whole dock for? You have'nt got a big ship there. There's lots of room for you".

Caldwell was pretty mad at that point, but brought the ship in very slowly and made a beautiful landing, with the ship's stem coming to within a few feet of the passenger ship ahead. There was still not sufficient room, our ship's stern touching the freighter and causing some damage to both. As soon as we had a gangway out the captain strode ashore and grabbed a piece of 2"x 4". Standing there was the American naval commander in charge of the dock, giving orders and watching everything. Captain Caldwell went over to him brandishing his 2"x 4".

"So we Canadians don't know how to berth a ship. I'll show you blankety-blank Americans".

The last I saw of the two of them was the American commander in full retreat with Captain Caldwell chasing after him, and "Tubby" Bryant, the third mate, up on the forecastle calling after him, "go get him, Cap". This all caused a lot of laughter among the longshoremen on the dock, and those of us on the ship who witnessed the incident.

The PRINCE RUPERT was quite an unlucky ship with several strandings and at least one sinking to her credit during her career. While I was aboard we had one strand but without serious damage. We had some near misses though, very much due to navigating in wartime conditions.

Eunice and young Danny by now had moved off Saltspring Island and were living with her parents in West Vancouver. This was much better from my point of view as it saved that long slog over to Saltspring every time I was able to spend some time at home.

Invariably they were to be seen by me, waiting and waving from the top landing at the C.N.R. docks when we arrived on a Monday.

My spell in passenger ships was an interesting break of eight months, but tugs were my life and I decided at the first opportunity to return to them, which resulted in me being appointed mate in the tug STANDON owned by Standard Towing Company, and it was in tugs that I spent the remainder of my career.

Chapter Seven

Towboating in Earnest

I joined the STANDON as mate. Standard Towing had a fleet of boats with similar names such as STANDTO, STANDFAST, STANDBY and so on. She carried a skipper, mate and cook-deckhand and was powered by a high speed diesel. She mostly did harbour work and the towing of logs out of Howe Sound to the mills in Burrard Inlet and the Fraser River, with occasional longer trips to Toba Inlet for flat booms.

Being quite small the accomodation was very restricted, the skipper occupying an open space alongside the companion way from the wheelhouse to the galley. The mate and deckhand had a bunk either side of the open forepeak ahead of the engine. The "heads" were off the engineroom, and, to enter, one had to go past the engine with all its exposed parts, pulleys and so forth, which required care. In fact later when I was master, the mate had a nasty accident when his pants leg was caught and he got his leg badly gashed so that we had to get him to hospital.

The owner of Standard Towing Ltd. was McKeen & Wilson Ltd., a holding company controlled by Senator Stan McKeen and the Wilson family, to whom I was not related in any way. At that time McKeen was busy organising Straits Towing Ltd. which emerged as one of the few very large towboat companies on the coast, and for many years was in quite a dominant position along with Island Tug & Barge, and Vancouver Tugboat Company Ltd. which could have been termed the "big three" in the fifties. Island Tug and Vancouver Tugboat Company eventually came together as Seaspan while Straits was to become one of the merging partners in Rivtow Straits, about which developments, more later.

The dealings and developments involving Senator McKeen and his associates had little effect on people within the company like myself, but after Straits was formed, Pacific Coyle Navigation, one of the bigger companies of the pre-war era was absorbed, in the early fifties, followed by Union Steamships of B.C. in the late fifties. I suppose it could be said that these moves marked the beginning of the seldom quiet process of merger and reorganisation within coastal towing, which continued unabated until the early eighties.

During this time I also did a trip in one of their bigger boats, the BELLE, before returning to the STANDON as mate, and after a few months, I became her master. Shortly afterwards STANDON was stationed at Gibsons. Her new job was to keep the Burns & Jackson Logging Company's booming grounds at Roberts Creek and Wilson Creek clear of sections of boomed logs, because they had so little capacity for holding inventories. Roberts Creek would hold four sections and Wilson Creek seven. We would normally go through to Wilson Creek, pick up what had accumulated there, add the Roberts Creek sections, and then tow them into the Howe Sound storage grounds. Timing was needed as we had to get into both booming grounds when there was sufficient water, as they either dried out or became very shallow. Then there was the matter of weather, as once having left Wilson Creek, a boat had to run for Shoal Channel entrance as quickly as possible. That short strip of coast was no place to be with a slow towing boom when the weather came up. In fact, there was simply no shelter anywhere.

One thing a young master runs up against is the unreasonable demands of the inexperienced layman, who may be good at running an army detachment, as happened in Prince Rupert when I served in the Army Transport Service boats, or later when a successful logger demanded safe and immediate removal of his logs, irrespective of the weather. Tugboat managers know that it is far less harmful to the corporate balance sheet to miss a tide and live for another day than to take foolish risks and lose a boat and perhaps a crew as well. Oh yes, I know that it is fashionable in certain quarters to be rated as a "hi-baller' and I equally know that a master must stand his ground even if the customer thinks he may be "yellow" for not going against his better judgement.

I had just such an incident with the late Mr. Jackson of Burns & Jackson of Roberts Creek. His company was an important operator and major contractor for McMillan Bloedel, although at this time I think they were still independent. They were also an important customer of Standard Towing, whom no tugboat company would want to sacrifice due to poor performance on the part of any of its own boats or people.

In this case we went into Wilson Creek with a rising westerly and two other tows in sight moving down coast off Roberts Creek. They were exerting everything to get into the shelter of Shoal Channel. As usual Mr. Jackson was standing by to see his logs off, and became quite angry when I said that I was going to wait for weather. Things were getting pretty acrimonious and tempers somewhat overheated, so I said,

"Very well, I'll tow your logs, as long as you assume full responsibility and will put that in writing".

He said he would, so I wrote out my version of a "hold harmless" agreement and got him to sign it, and off we went with seven sections into worsening weather. It was very bouncy out there, and while the boat was not in any particular danger, logs kept popping out from inside the boomsticks. When we got down to Shelter Island, opposite Gibsons, there was not much left, so when I saw Mr. Jackson I told him that most of what I still had were his boom sticks! There was nothing he could say as he strode off without a word, but I guess he learned that he should never override the judgement of the skipper unless he was prepared to shoulder full responsibility. When I spoke by phone to the dispatcher he was pretty upset by my first news regarding the loss of logs, but very happy when I told him the full story and added that I held a hold harmless agreement, which head office was pretty anxious to receive from me.

I think it is true to say that in the late forties and early fifties, with new postwar operators getting into both towing and logging, matters in log towing on the coast were pretty chaotic, with poorly constructed booms, underpowered boats, inexperienced towboat personnel, sloppy management and wholesale thieving of logs out of the booming grounds. The insurance companies were staggering under the burden of claims, and of course there was no gain to be made if a tugboat or its owner got a bad reputation with insurers, and without a doubt this did happen with some of them. The result was the formation of the Gulf Log Salvage Co-operative Association, made up of representatives from the logging and insurance industries.

Common standards were eventually adopted in making up booms and towing arrangements, surveying boats to be sure of their fitness for the job, surveying booms to make sure that they were correctly assembled and fit to be towed, approval of booming grounds by Gulf Log Salvage and similar safeguards, and without these standards it became impossible to buy insurance on log booms. Another important outgrowth of this was to license beachcombers, with the proceeds of all salvage logs going into a pool were the proceeds could be returned to the rightful owners, and insurance losses reduced, while still ensuring a fair return for the beachcomber.

The arrangement for employing the STANDON out of Gibsons continued for about a year, so I rented a cottage on the Gibsons waterfront and moved Eunice and Danny over. This property had its own dock which was big enough to take the STANDON, so in effect I had my charge right in my own front yard on standby for anything needed when I was not towing out of Wilson Creek. When things were quiet and the weather good as happened from time to time, I used to gather the family and a small group of friends together and take the STANDON up to West Bay on Gambier Island to check booms and have a picnic or swim. Mind you I always made certain that we had sufficient life-jackets available for the two or three extra we carried!

One mishap which we did have involved the shallow underwater ridge in Shoal Channel which runs between Keats Island and Georgia Bluffs at Gibsons. It is sufficiently shallow to preclude larger boats crossing it, and even with smaller boats if the height of the tide was insufficient, it sometimes meant going around the east side of Keats Island into Collingwood Channel, in order to make an entrance into the log storage grounds on Gambier Island. In this instance a towboat was in need of assistance on the outside, having dropped its propeller to the south of the Trail Islands with a strong westerly blowing, and we were on our way out to help her. By the time we got off Gower Point, it was obvious that seas there were more than our small boat could safely handle, so I managed to turn her around and headed back into Shoal Channel. I knew that the depth of water made things a little chancy, but decided to risk it. As the swells caused by the waves outside came surging in we touched ground just once with a single bump, and I lost my steering. We put the lifeboat overside and filled her with sufficient water, to create a drogue which enabled us to steer sufficiently well and make Gibsons harbour. An examination revealed that we had lost our rudder and shoe, and we had to be towed into Vancouver for repairs.

Another incident involving the STANDON occurred when we were called out to look for a fish boat that had gone aground in heavy fog at Calamity Light in the First Narrows. We found her and pulled her off, and by that time there was another fishboat ashore between Siwash Rock and Prospect Point which again we located. This was a bigger boat, a fairly large seiner of 60 feet or more, and while attending to her we got a further call from our office to say that yet a third boat had gone aground on the mud flats near Brockton Point. We replied and said that we would deal with her on our way in.

Meanwhile the master of the second boat asked us if he could follow us in. I said that would be fine, but told him that once abreast of Calamity Light he should keep going straight ahead to go up the harbour, and not follow me as I had to feel my way over the mud flats past Brockton Point to assist the third fishboat. He said he understood me, so we moved in through the Narrows and very quickly I lost sight of him, although it seems he could probably still see my wake. As we came abreast of Brockton Point we took way off, and moved in following the shore line over the flats with the mate taking soundings continuously.

I could hear number three banging on metal of some sort and eased back as I moved in towards him while making voice contact, I was taking soundings and was at my limit without grounding, when next thing I knew, I could hear the "thunkety-thunk" of a diesel engine coming up astern. It was our overly friendly second boat, the seiner who had disregarded what I had told him and continued to follow us like a pet dog. I could see number three boat about fifty feet away from our present position laying there on the mud. Number two fortunately drew more water than we did, which slowed him down as his keel slid over the mud, just before he hit us and knocked the STANDON herself firmly aground.

But for this we would have been able to feel our way in, and reach number three with a line, but now the net result was one tug and two fishboats ashore, all at the same spot. It was all pretty embarrassing, so I called the office and told them what had happened and soon another tug was on its way to get us off again. Fortunately we had suffered no damage as he had lost most of his way when he came into contact with us.

The thing to keep in mind here, is that while radar had been developed and was in general use on warships and other large vessels, it was not yet available and in general use among our towboat and fishboat fleet. We still had to rely greatly on our own senses, overstrained eyes, finely tuned hearing, echo bouncing and even on occasion smell, to feel our way around. The reader will remember the classic story earlier in this narrative when a dog's bark was even crucial to navigation in one narrow pass on the coast. In the final analysis, local knowledge was probably the most critical factor of all. Experienced towboat masters stored this up in their own private way, many like me developing copious notes of everything I saw and learned as I progressed around the coast. Also there was a kind of brotherhood on the coast as anyone who listened into marine radio conversations between boat and boat, would hear masters swapping information with each other on weather, sea conditions, some hazard that had been noted, and special things to watch out for when entering some remote anchorage.

I was fortunate in the year that I was towing between Wilson and Roberts Creeks as the only time I had a loss of logs was the occasion I have already recounted, when I lost the Burns & Jackson logs, having gone out very much against my better judgement.

Another occasion I remember very well was when the STANDON was acting as an "assist" boat on a boom going up the Fraser River. This tow was in charge of old Captain Louie Larsen, a well known old-timer towboat master. For the uninitiated, an assist boat is used rather like an extra locomotive when a train is going through the mountains. All it really involves is the temporary addition of more power to "assist" when a towboat is racing to get its tow into safe waters, for example as so often happens after being caught south of the Trail Islands heading for Howe Sound, in the face of oncoming worsening weather.

In this case, we were mainly there to take control of the tail end of the tow to prevent it hanging up on other booms or vessels and the river banks themselves, under flood tide conditions, always of course taking directions over the radio telephone from the leading tug. Everything was going alright when we had to slow down for other tugs in the river, so I eased off until the lead tug asked for full power again. As we slowed the flood tide current caught the boom and before I knew it we were aground and pulling over as the boom surged ahead on the current.

The vessel was at such an acute angle, in fact almost on her beam ends and in danger of filling. The quickest way off the bridge was to simply walk down the side of the house. I grabbed a fireaxe and chopped our now overly taught line free. As soon as we relieved the pressure she righted herself but I was firmly aground and had to relay the news to Captain Larsen at the head of the boom. We came off as the tide came in, with nothing worse than our pride a little hurt! Afterwards my footsteps, like those of a human fly, could be seen quite easily, on the white house sides, and might have been the cause of a little curiosity to anyone who saw them.

Time off in those days was very hit and miss, and when times were slack the crew would be given any time off that could be managed. Several times when living in Gibsons, I would have to go over to Shelter Island to check booms tied up there, so would take Eunice along as crew. I would be out on the booms and would give her instructions as to what I wanted her to do with the boat, pushing here and pulling there, and then bringing the boat around to a new position. She was a natural ship handler and had no difficulty in doing exactly what I asked her, which sometimes is a little harder to achieve with a regular so-called experienced crewman as I found out on a number of occasions.

I do recall one character we had on board. He was a very excitable French-Canadian who had some difficulty with English. One day we were passing through Shoal Channel and I wanted him on the winch to shorten up. I called him out of the galley where he was busy munching on an apple. He started the winch up and began to shorten up on the towline. When we had as much line in as I wanted I called down to him, "stop her up, Frenchy", but it was as though he had not heard. A second order to "stop her" brought no response and by this time we were not far off dragging the boom right up on to our stern. The third time I saw him take something out of his mouth and throw it over the side, but this time he put the hydraulic gear out and applied the winch brake. He then had to let line out as the boom was far too close for safety's sake. When it was all over I called him to come up on the flying bridge and I asked him what the problem had been.

"Well, I got all excited and put the apple I was eating in my mouth to be able to use both hands and could not answer your question, and in frustration grabbed the apple and threw it overboard with my false teeth still in it!", he replied in his strongly French accent.

I had became interested in the Vancouver Barge Transportation service into Gibsons, whose covered barge called three times a week with freight in tow of their tug TRUCILLA, a 110 foot long ex-U.S. Navy vessel. This seemed like an interesting alternative to log towing around the Sunshine Coast, so I called Vancouver

Diesel tug TRUCILLA
One of two sisters. former U.S. sub-catchers and the author's first command after obtaining his masters certificate.

Barge to see if they had any openings for a mate. Sure enough they did have an opening and wanted to hire me. I said my thankyous and goodbyes to Standard Towing and a few days later joined the TRUCILLA as mate.

As befitted a former submarine chaser from the first world war, the TRUCILLA was long and lean. The master had his cabin on the upper deck astern of the wheelhouse with an outside toilet, and the funnel astern of the master's cabin. Six of the crew were housed on the lower main deck, which was entered through the foc'sle, so, as mate, I had my own cabin astern of the galley, as did the two engineers, two quartermasters and the cook. The four deckhands had lower main deck fo'c'sle type quarters aft of the engine room. The entire crew, totalling eleven, shared a nice large messroom. This was the largest crew I had sailed with as mate and we were on a six-hour watch system, except for the deckhands whose main duty was working cargo.

Vancouver Barge Transportation tugs were really almost small freighters towing their barge behind them. The company was not related in any way to the far larger Vancouver Tugboat Company, even though there were Lindsays in both concerns, but here again they were unrelated. The company prospered as a scheduled freight carrier delivering dry cargo of every description, including heavy equipment, animal feed and hay together with groceries and parcels to Gibsons, Half Moon Bay, Pender Harbour, Stillwater as far north as Powell River and from there across to Courtenay to the company's own dock. Some time later, in order to speed things, a small local tug would come down river and exchange our barge for an empty one so that we could then head south without delay. Going south we called in at Blubber Bay and Vananda, and loaded crushed limestone products for Vancouver. As the road and ferry system improved, this whittled away at their business until they eventually sold out in the fifties to Vancouver Tugboat Company, probably for relatively little money, as most of the equipment was not too well-fitted for other employment.

In those times we worked seven days per week, accumulating Sundays, and thus getting one week off in seven. Pay was quite low by today's standards, although it must not be forgotten that a dollar in 1945 would buy an awful lot compared to today. A deckhand, for example, would make up to $60 per month, while a mate such as I was, would earn around $125-135 per month. At Vancouver we were loaded by longshoremen, but until the barge returned to Vancouver, the work was heavy and demanding and by today's standards needlessly so, the heavy labour being provided by the four deckhands, using simple two-wheel handtrucks.

This was reasonably straightforward while the tide was high enough to maintain the barge at a suitable level alongside the dock, thus permitting easy running over the ramp, but if the tide was low, the ramp became too steep to permit wheeling the handcarts up with their loads. As the barge fell on a receding tide, we opened up a roof hatch which was in effect a continuation of the side opening door so that the barge house looked as though it had had a slice removed in much the same way as taking a segment out of a cake. When the tide was low, we then had to rig a snatch block on the dock and run the tug's cargo winch through it with a sleigh hook on the end. The hand truck axles would be hooked on to it and the truck and crewman pulled up the steep plank upon a signal to the engineer running the winch. The returning crewman and truck would hook in and pull the line back for the next waiting load.

With this arrangement we managed to work cargo effectively but perhaps a little crudely. It was hardly a safe practice, but we managed to get along without any serious injuries. This was a far cry from some years later when I was master on a similar service provided by Island Tug to Northern Vancouver Island ports, where the far larger barge used was provided with forklifts and an elevator.

The TRUCILLA and her sister ETTA MAC were very good seaboats even though they rolled a lot on account of their narrow beam. They were nice and easy in a following sea which made them near-ideal for the service in which they were used. Regularity is synonymous with reliability in operating a scheduled freight service, and I cannot recall any occasion when we were delayed on account of weather. In those days we had no gyro compasses, radar or depth sounders. Navigation was all done by dead reckoning and when I look back it is remarkable how we managed to stay out of serious trouble, particularly considering the boiler like pressure everyone lived with on a daily basis in maintaining the service.

In the spring of 1945, I figured it was about time that I obtained my home trade master's certificate, and I told Vancouver Barge that I needed six weeks off to go to the Navigation school. This was a private operation run by a Captain Norman Young, assisted by two instructors, Captain George Murrell, and a retired Canadian National master, Captain Dougie Graham. Eunice and I would sit around the table at home while she tested me on just about everything I had to know from rules of the road, to navigation, through to ship handling and a host of other subjects.

Vancouver Barge called me every so often to find out when I would be back. Each time I had to tell them what they already knew, which was that the course required six weeks and there was really no possible short cut. I went before the examiner of masters and mates, Captain Patrick, a very dour little man who had been to sea in sail and had ended up as a master in the Canadian Pacific "Empresses". He called everyone "Laddie" whether you were a young fellow in your twenties or well into your sixties. He went over my papers and about half way through said it was obvious that I had more than enough sea time. I went in to write my exams which started on the Monday and continued through to Friday, with Vancouver Barge continuing to call almost by the day, but I was not going to be put off by their pressure.

The marking was done right away and I was told to come back at three in the afternoon to be told if I had passed or failed. I verbally received my results and got the good news that I had passed. I phoned Vancouver Barge immediately and told them I had passed, so they said,

"That's great, we want you to sail tonight as master on the TRUCILLA".

I contacted Captain Patrick and explained my predicament to him, as I needed my certificate right away. His attitude at first was that whatever I had on my mind could be held over until Monday as he was on his way home for the weekend. Quite apart from that, certificates came from Ottawa and would not reach me for a week or more.

This was the voice of officialdom, but he could see I was disappointed when I told him I had been offered a command to start that evening, so he replied,

"That is sure a quick promotion is'nt it?", with which of course I agreed. He carried on, "I'll tell you what, laddie, I like your attitude and you've got good marks, so I will give you a temporary permit and number and that will look after you until your ticket comes through". This attested to the fact that I had passed the examination for home trade master, and that my permanent certificate would follow in due course.

After this I went home and celebrated with Eunice and her family for a couple of hours. I do recall saying to Eunice, "It's too bad that you did'nt have your sea time in, as you could easily have passed", and I'm sure she could as she had, and still has a wonderful memory for storing up knowledge, quite apart from the fact that she was used to being around boats. In joining the TRUCILLA, I knew that there were a number of things that I would want to change from my days as mate, but then of course I was not in a position to do anything much about them. I called the crew together and let them know what I expected of them from hereon, just so that we would get on a proper footing from the beginning. They all had their jobs for which they were responsible, and I expected them to be dealt with diligently at all times. One mistake was forgivable, but if they did not learn from that and correct it, the second time it was repeated they would be off the boat.

Some of the crew members whom I remember very well aboard the TRUCILLA, were Walter Gordy and his twin brother Harry. Walter eventually went into the B.C. Pilotage Service, but his brother was lost overboard from the ISLAND MARINER when it was on charter to Vancouver Barge and I do not believe his body was ever found. What happened, from what I understand, was that he was back aft to shorten up the tow line to go through Coal Island Pass after leaving what is now Schwartz Bay Ferry Terminal. The ISLAND MARINER, being a steamer, had a large winch. On this winch when the deckhand put the brake on, he took a bar and placed it through the spoked wheel pulling very hard to cinch it up as tight as possible.

The only thing they can think happened was that while he was bearing down, the bar slipped out of the wheel, causing him to lose his footing, and plunge overside leaving his cap and cigarette package on the deck. Walter was mate at the time and had sent his brother aft to deal with the winch, expecting him to report back momentarily that everything was secure aft. It was a nasty experience for Walter to find his twin brother had been lost. They were both fine young men, and Walter went on to become an equally fine mariner for the rest of his working life.

Another young fellow who came on during his summer leaves as a crewman was Johnny Antle, the grandson of the Reverend John Antle, who did such a lot with church mission boats over many years. Our second engineer was Thor Larsen who went on to establish tugboat companies with his brother Bert, probably the best known of their operations being Service Tugboats of North Vancouver, until it was sold to Weldwood Ltd. Gordy Willis came on as my mate, and proved to be a real asset so far as I was concerned as he was a first rate ship handler. Colin Longmuir was another very reliable man who came aboard, whom I had known when he was a lookout on the C.N.R. ships. All in all we had a very fine crew who worked together in harmony with virtually no crew changes, which surely must be a good sign from both the vessel owner's and the master's point of view.

I had a few things I was determined to sort out with the office. The quality of "grub" coming aboard left a lot to be desired. There was no problem with packaged foods of course but the meat was terrible stuff. Fresh fruit and vegetables were very far from fresh, and obviously purchased with an eye to the utmost economy, by someone who ignored the fact that lousy food was the quickest way to create discontent among a crew, particularly one like ours whose output of work was expected to be about the highest that a human could perform.

I took some of this junk meat up to the office and left it on the manager's desk, it being the weekend with no one around upstairs. They were not too happy when they came in on Monday. The place smelled as though something had died there and to top if off they saw my note, which said I hoped they enjoyed eating this stuff, because we certainly could not aboard the TRUCILLA. He called me in to give me a dressing down, but I stood my ground and got a little angry in the process, telling him a few other hometruths about matters which needed rectifying on the boats.

This created quite a hullabaloo, but it did have the effect of seeing some improvements made in the quality of what we had delivered to the boats. Another thing I was not happy about was the quality of the paint. It again was very poor stuff which chalked as soon as it dried, and it really was a waste of time and money putting it on. I complained to the same manager when he came down to the boat, but he replied that they were not going to change anything, and what they supplied would continue. I managed to back him up against the bulkhead so that his back was in contact with dry, chalky paint, and as he stepped ashore I said,

"If you care to turn around and take a look at your jacket, you'll see what I mean. Most of the paint is on your back now as chalk which proves my point. It'll wash off the first time we take a sea or are in rain".

I had made my point. He stormed off following this conversation, however the next time paint was delivered to the ship it was a different brand and better quality! As they say "penny wise and pound foolish", although it is a lesson in simple economics that some vessel owners never learn.

One other incident worth recalling concerns the Canadian Merchant Service Guild. In this instance the TRUCILLA was laying at the Vancouver Barge Dock near the Buckerfield elevator. This dock was a private facility with a gateman who had the power to keep "undesirables" out. The Guild representatives told the gateman their business and were turned away. When I learned of this I phoned the Guild and said that if they wanted to come aboard they should contact me ahead of time, so that I could put the boat into Buckerfield's dock. In fact, I told them that if they wanted to come down now, I would move TRUCILLA over to Buckerfields right away, which is exactly what I did. The Guild men came down and we listened to what they had to say.

Vancouver Barge at that time had no union agreements aboard their vessels. However, the marine employees were certainly looking for better conditions and with good reason. When the office heard of this, they had me up on the carpet again, and made it clear that I must have their permission which I knew would not be granted. I told them in turn that if I wanted to invite people aboard, that was my right as master of the vessel, and nothing would change that so far as I was concerned!

Another incident occurred during the annual fishing event organised by Mr. Wilson, General Manager of VBT, when five or six businessmen friends were carried aboard TRUCILLA from Vancouver to Nelson Island to enjoy some lake fishing.

We departed as usual on our northern run at 8 p.m. with a stop at Gibsons, worked cargo and carried on again. Our passengers were playing cards in the galley when we departed, but at about two in the morning I was called by the mate to say that there was so much row coming out of the galley, the off-duty crew could not sleep.

Upon getting dressed and going below, I found a noisy card game in progress with booze on the table which was obviously being consumed at a rapid rate. I asked Mr. Wilson to pack it up and gave him a good reason. This was a working ship where men had to be up and refreshed to do a full day's work. He replied that in his position he could do as he liked, and that I should go back to bed. At that point we were just passing Sechelt, so I told them, that if any further noise was made I would have them all removed at the Sechelt government dock, and then I departed for my bunk. There were no further crew complaints and three hours later we disembarked our passengers at Nelson Island, without a word being spoken between us.

On our return south the next day, we picked up our fishermen again and had an uneventful trip back with no reference at all to the incident of the previous day. In disembarking at Vancouver, one of the guests, the late Mr. Ernie Buckerfield, one of Vancouver's best known businessmen of the day, thanked me for carrying them. He gave me his card, and said that if there were any repercussions over my actions to please let him know as he considered I had handled the situation correctly. I never heard anything further about the incident!

On another occasion I was called into the office by Mr. George Lindsey. This time the atmosphere was a lot better. He knew that I had lived in the Gulf Islands and had previously run a freight service through the islands knowing all the various small ports and landings. He said they were looking into starting a service through the islands and wanted me to take leave from the TRUCILLA, renew old aquaintances and see what the possibilities were.

Off I went and travelled through all the areas I knew to be dependent on water transportation for their supplies. At this time the only freight service from the mainland was by the C.P.R. passenger steamer PRINCESS MARY. She had limited time on her passenger schedule for freight, and not too much space for carrying it. In fully explaining how VBT handled the northern freight and the Victoria service, and discussing a proposed schedule for the islands, the reception I received was strong enough for Mr. Lindsey to justify a service. I rejoined the TRUCILLA as master and soon we were transferred to this new run.

It was decided to depart for the islands on Mondays, Wednesdays and Fridays, when loading was completed around 8 p.m. We would sail directly to Nanaimo and worked cargo for 2-3 hours, and from there we passed through Dodds Narrows to Thetis Island. At this point we would travel with the barge alongside to save time in not having to pick it up continuously in all our landings.

The next stop would be Kuper Island Indian School followed by Chemainus with three separate dockings. Then we carried on to Vesuvius Bay, Burgoyne Bay, Musgraves Landing, Cowichan Bay, Fulford Harbour, Beaver Point, Port Washington, Lyall Harbour, Ganges, Montague Harbour, Mayne Island and Galiano Island.

These stops, depending on cargo, had anywhere from 15 minutes to two hours for working cargo. We carried everything from groceries to heavy machinery, trucks, tons of feed and building supplies etc. We returned usually with fresh produce and general cargo. This run proved to be most successful in terms of cargo moved and filling a need, but the list of points of call recited above will give an indication of the speed at which we moved, and needless to say it was very stressful and hard on both the crew and the vessel.

The watchkeepers maintained their six hours on and six hours off, with the deckhands working cargo at each stop. I was most fortunate in having Gordon Willis, formerly of the PRINCE RUPERT, as my mate. He was a top boat handler and was able to make landings under normal conditions on his own watch. Also Walter Gordy and Colin Longmuir served as quartermasters who could handle the necessary duties in the wheelhouse. With some stops only being 15 minutes to an hour apart, the mate and the master would be dead on their feet in no time.

Before leaving Vancouver Barge, a few other instances will help illustrate the hectic nature of working for a scheduled freight barge line.

The main engine in the TRUCILLA was a direct reversible, and from "stop", the engineer would move the cams to the ahead or astern position according to the order. Then he would press a small handle against the air start button and hold it there until the engine was running on diesel fuel. In this instance, I was turning the vessel in a very confined space by backing and filling to get alongside my barge and had backed off and stopped and then had ordered "half ahead" with hard port helm intending to go "half astern" again for the last back and fill. Upon ordering "stop", all went well, but on the following "half astern"nothing happended, so I rang for "full astern" as we were heading for the centre of the barge which longshoremen were loading. I heard a yell, and on looking aft I saw the chief engineer running up the deck towards the wheelhouse waving something. I sounded several short blasts on the whistle to let the people on the barge know that we were about to ram, which we did, hitting her with a heavy glancing blow. Luckily no one was injured and no serious damage was done to either the barge or our tug. What happened was that the chief engineer had pushed the lever for the air button start astern, and the handle broke off, so that he had no way of giving the engine the needed air pressure for starting.

Another time we were laying alongside our barge and not expecting to move in to reload for 2-3 hours, so I let the crew who wanted to, go uptown to buy cigarettes etc. We ended up with just Gordie Willis and myself on board when we had orders to move along the dock to the other berth. I took up my usual position on the barge, and Gordie was in the wheelhouse as usual tending to both the steering and engine-room telegraph as required. I would call an order and he would answer me and run to the engine room and start or stop the engine as needed, and then race back to the wheelhouse. This went on for several moves and eventually I had her safely tied up and loading started. No one ashore really noticed how we had done it, or that we had accomplished it with just two of us aboard!

After we had tied up, I discussed with Gordie as to how things had gone with him, and he laughingly told me that when an engine room order came through he rang the telegraph for the order, tore down to the engine-room, answered the order back to the wheelhouse, dealt with the engine and then raced back into the wheelhouse to resume taking the helm. He was a real joker and I doubled up with laughter as I now remembered hearing the engine room bells ringing and never gave it a thought!

A near miss involving possible death or serious injury by crushing between the barge and the tug, occurred when approaching our barge at the Gibsons wharf for a port-to landing. I was approaching in the usual manner, with the tug's bow heading on an angle to the barge so that when I went astern as the way was taken off, the stern would pull in, ending up flat alongside. Despite all safety instructions that no person jump across from the tug to the barge before the vessel had all way off, a seaman decided to make the four foot jump from the bow of the tug to the barge. TRUCILLA had just started to go "half astern" so that the gap was widening and the man fell into the water between the two vessels. An instant decision was made to go ahead again and to go over to hard aport so as to throw our hull away from him and the barge. We saved him without injury but hit the dock which was right ahead of us breaking several piles, which was better than having a crushed crewman. Needless to say he almost learned the hard way to think and to obey orders before jumping.

With a brand new barge which had not had maximum tonnage aboard as yet, we got orders when coming southbound out of Courtenay for Vancouver to stop at Vananda on Texada Island and take a capacity load of crushed limerock in 100 lb. sacks. Having an approximate tonnage displacement load for this barge, we started to load during my watch. Upon being relieved by Gordie Willis at noon, I told him what tonnage we should try for and also the minimum required freeboard fore and aft that I wanted regardless of tonnage. I woke up about three hours later and heard the loading still going on, got up and asked the mate what his tonnage was. The barge had far more freeboard than the tonnage would allow so I told him to stop loading while I checked some figures.

Nothing worked out or made any sense, but suddenly it dawned on me. I checked the tide book and we were loading on an extreme low tide which was now rising so we sat and waited for the tide to lift the barge which was sitting there with far more of a load than normal. When the barge floated the freeboard was scary, with less than a foot forward and about two inches aft. I did not want to unload, so upon checking with the weather station decided to leave. Fortunately the weather was perfect all the way down and we made it without mishap. I was asked by Mr. Wilson what tonnage we had on board and told him that we had a maximum load for good weather and suggested freeboards for normal conditions and added that we just wanted to see what she would carry on this trial trip! He was quite pleased until he saw the freeboard but never discussed it further with me.

On another occasion when picking up our barge in a south east gale at Comox, a bridle became tangled up in our propeller. We contacted a nearby river tug which took the barge off us and towed us to the government dock. I noticed the tide was high and checked the tide tables, finding it was a large ebb. I figured that rather than get everyone excited at the Vancouver office, I would slide TRUCILLA up the side of the dock inshore until she touched bottom, wait for her to become dry, cut the bridle out, refloat with the next incoming tide and then be on our way. All went well with only an entry in the log book, no tow, no divers and no drydock costs, with only a few hours lost time!

One day in thick fog we were departing from Thetis Island with the barge alongside. We had backed up on our back spring to get the compass heading I wanted to proceed for a specific number of minutes for a whistle echo off an island ahead, where I had a severe turn to port around a rock to go between it and the island. I then had to run a few minutes again for another port steering alteration to head into the Kuper Island dock for whistle echoes and a landing. The tide was running quite hard to the south and set me more to port than I had allowed for, and in making my turn and running at half speed, I felt the tug's bow start to rise. I stopped engines but the barge's momentum kept us moving. We rolled slightly to starboard, then the stern came up perceptibly and moments later we regained an even keel. I knew that we had touched and gone over the outer edge of the rock, and the barge having a shallower draft had simply sailed over it without touching. I put the engines "slow ahead" and then "half ahead" with no vibration and no problem with steering so carried on with our trip with no apparent damage. Upon the vessel's next drydocking there was slight scarring on the port lower bilge and keel with no attention required!

The final episode I would like to recount concerns the time we left Nanaimo for Comox in a south east gale with heavy snow. I turned the watch over to the mate at 2400 hours with visibility at about a quarter of a mile and a heavy sea running astern.

I awoke on my own at about 0200, to hear the whistle sounding and the ship rolling heavily, so I got up and went into the wheelhouse. I was uneasy about the way the vessel was rolling with that heavy southeaster. It did not feel right, so I checked the compass heading, and questioned the mate on his courses and position, but it did not make sense to me. I turned the light on in the wheelhouse after asking the quartermaster if he had a knife or metal in his pockets, and in looking around found a flashlight on the shelf under the compass. Upon removing it, the compass adjusted back about two and a half points. We got her back to where the seas felt about right and allowed a further adjustment to port to make up for the false deviation caused by the flashlight. We proceeded cautiously along our way until we picked up the fog horn at the entrance to Baynes Sound. This was another lesson fortunately without serious consequences, and of course the truth is that one just never knows when other people may do things that affect the safety of the vessel. Sometimes it is just too late to avoid trouble if one finds out after the fact.

However the time was coming close when I felt I was ready to go into business for myself, and that is how Dola Towing Company and Associated Tugboats came into being, and are now the subject of the next chapter.

Chapter Eight

Dola Towing and Associated Tugboats Ltd.

By 1946 business was showing many signs of returning to a peacetime economy. The feverish activity in the local shipyards which was the focus of much of the visible local war effort, was now starting to subside, servicemen were returning to civilian jobs and overall there was a considerable spirit of optimism about the future of Canada and the prosperity which would be ours in the balance of the twentieth century.

Much local talk so far as I was concerned also focused on the future of the forest industries with Canadian lumber being exported overseas as fast as it could be milled, particularly to Britain and war-torn Europe. A sizeable shipowning industry sprang up based on Vancouver and Montreal in particular, with a substantial fleet of wartime 10,000 ton freighters, formerly owned by a crown company called Park Steamships Ltd., but now under the control of private owners. Of the total, no less than 44 of these ships, at the peak of activity, called Vancouver their home port with almost all being engaged in loading out full cargoes of B.C. lumber, pulp, paper and prairie grain exports. Supplying the pulp and paper mills, of which there were a much smaller number than there are now, and keeping the logs moving from the camps to the sawmills, played a very big part in the early prosperity of the towboat industry.

Optimism and a newfound peacetime prosperity was a fresh experience for me, as it will be remembered that I first went to sea in 1933, at the age of 14, which was at just about the height of the depression, and so far as Western Canada was concerned economic activity and a reasonable level of employment were still a long way off most ideas of prosperity, when war broke out in 1939.

I had been fortunate, I suppose, in that I had managed to remain gainfully employed ever since leaving school in 1933, and each move I made had generally been a progressive one in which I gained much sea time and practical experience.

By 1945 I had achieved my first command of a regular commercial vessel in the coastwise trade. Danny, our oldest son, now 4 years old, was joined in that year by our second son, Ted. His arrival completed our family.

Being 27, and I suppose having all the drive and ambition of a young, perhaps at times restless family man with an eye to business, I was nurturing ideas of going into business for myself in towboating, which was the only industry of which I had experience, coupled with a strong desire to succeed.

By 1946 I had heard that Pacific Salvage Company Ltd. of North Vancouver wished to sell their steam tug DOLA, so I went over to see her laying at her berth in North Vancouver. Built as long ago as 1907, she was in quite a sorry state to look at, but she had the potential I felt I needed to get launched. I spoke with Mr. Don Greenwood of Pacific Salvage to find out what the company had in mind for a price, but the owner of the company, A.C. Burdick, was away for a couple of months and nothing could be settled until his return. This was a bit of a setback, but

Steam Tug DOLA
Ready to tow a log boom.

Steam Tug Dola
Ashore at Musgraves Landing.

Raising a family and starting a towboat company
Eunice, Ted Junior, Dan and Ted Senior.

it gave me the opportunity to look around and see what employment possibilities could be developed. I got talking with Mr. Greenwood who was very interested in my background and experience particularly with barge handling. He asked me if I would be interested in taking command of the SALVAGE CHIEFTAIN towing railcar barges for the Canadian Pacific Railway until Mr. Burdick's return.

I told him I would think it over and let him know the following day. It struck me as being an attractive idea, so with a phone call I was hired by Pacific Salvage and after familiarisation with the SALVAGE CHIEFTAIN sailed her over to the CPR dock to take my first railcar barge over to Nanoose Bay.

While master of the SALVAGE CHIEFTAIN I naturally became familiar with various departments of the C.P.R. and got to know Captain Jimmy Hamilton, Superintendent of their coast steamships at that time. In fact he accompanied us on several occasions while delivering barges to Nanoose Bay. Everyone knew that the SALVAGE CHIEFTAIN was a far bigger vessel than was actually needed on a run like this given the size of the barges we handled at that time. In fact it was obvious also that this was really an ideal run for a vessel like DOLA, but I held my own counsel until Mr. Burdick's return when we could see how the idea of our purchasing this tug would unfold. When Mr. Burdick returned, I managed to see him and was very well received. I guess Don Greenwood had helped by giving him a good

Diesel Tug SQUAMISH QUEEN
Another long serving barge towboat under charter to Dola on the Squamish railcar barge run.

report on me and my activities as master of the SALVAGE CHIEFTAIN. He confirmed what they had in mind for an asking price, which I do not now recall, but the upshot was that we agreed on a price of $25,000, with $10,000 down and the balance on terms. I asked him if their arrangements with the C.P.R. for the railcar barge run to Vancouver Island were long term, and he confirmed that they were not. In fact they were just helping the C.P.R. out on a fairly short term basis, and both he and the C.P. knew that they were employing a far bigger vessel than necessary, and quite part from that Pacific had no intention of getting into the general towing business. I asked him if he would have any objection to me approaching the C.P.R. with the idea of employing the DOLA, and he confirmed that he did not.

I spent quite a lot of time with Captain Hamilton and departments of the C.P.R. and visited such firms as, what was then called H.R. MacMillan Export Company. Bloedel Stewart & Welch, Kingcome Navigation and several of the big log towers. I enjoyed quite an encouraging reception, and with the C.P. as the first prize, things were looking quite promising.

With good employment prospects I next tackled the challenge of raising money. In those days $10,000 was a lot of money for a young towboat master with a family to support and only limited personal savings. In the Vancouver of 1946, $10,000 would have purchased a very fine family home, in many of the better parts of the city, for example. My father loaned me $2500 to get me started, then I chatted to Al Tufts who previously had sailed in the DOLA, and was interested in becoming a shareholder, as was Captain Murrell, my old instructor at the Government Navigation School for whom I had always had a high regard. Over the weekend I was chatting across the garden fence with Oliver Sloan, my neighbour in West Van-

Diesel Tug/Packer RANDY
Which gave long service to Dola in towing barges to Squamish.

Steam Tug LE ROI
Under charter to Dola Towing.

Diesel Tug SANTRINA
A modern unit of the Pacific Coyle Navigation Company, purchased like others from surplus U.S. Army vessels, following World War II. Later incorporated into the Straits Towing fleet.

couver. He was retired from the army and had been a businessman, and he likewise was keen to invest.

With these four initial shareholders including myself, we now had our $10,000 and thus organised Dola Towing Co. Ltd. After putting DOLA up on the drydock to make sure that everything was alright with the hull and underwater fittings, all arrangements for the purchase were completed with Mr. Burdick, and a line of credit established at Pacific Dry Dock Company, another one of the Burdick companies for anything we needed in putting DOLA back into commission. I also established a credit line with the Royal Bank with whom I had always dealt.

With the DOLA now having completed her refit and back in the water, we took her out into English Bay to swing her compasses, and then told the CPR that we now had the DOLA ready for business. It was then that I found to my surprise that C.P. had once owned her in earlier days.

Our first guaranteed work with them was a twice weekly tow to James Island with their C.P. No. 7, a nine car unit carrying tankcars and general cargo for the explosives plant of Canadian Industries Ltd. at James Island. This barge carried a crewman on board in a little doghouse aft. The routine was to go into the Village dock to unload general cargo boxcars and then go around the other side of the island opposite Saanichton to pump off tank car products, then return to the Village Dock to load returning cars filled with explosives for Vancouver. Interspersed with this regular run were periodic trips into Nanoose Bay and Ladysmith with an odd railcar barge delivery to Squamish for the Pacific Great Eastern Railway (PGE).

Steam Tug ISLAND MARINER
One of Island Tug's early steamers, formerly the quarantine vessel Madge, which Dola chartered.

This is where Eunice came into the picture again. She was at home and quite busy looking after the needs of our two small boys, but she had also become familiar with a number of the people we did business with. If I found that we had two or three slack days coming up, I would call her on the radiophone and ask her to call "So-and-so" to find out if his company had any jobs open. She would call me in the evening as we had a regular standby time for this purpose. Eunice's efforts might result in a tow to Powell River for the Powell River Company with an empty barge up, and a returned loaded barge for example, so that in effect her role quickly became that of dispatcher for Dola Towing, and a job which I could clearly not handle myself as I was fulltime master of the DOLA.

Another slot we were able to fill was in our accounting. Harry Roberts, Eunice's younger brother, had returned from overseas service and was now at U.B.C. taking a bachelor of commerce degree, so working part time for us he was able to set up a proper accounting system, and then, having obtained his degree, he came into the company full time which was great from our point of view as the business was growing all the time.

Maintaining schedules so that we could look after our number one customer, the CPR, sometimes became quite harrowing, particularly on the James Island run with frequent heavy fog to contend with. As always a bad spot was Active Pass, and while we did not have the heavy ferry traffic of today, we did have frequent CPR passenger ships to contend with on their Vancouver-Victoria run, plus the overnight boat, and others of that fleet maintaining their triangular run which included Seattle. We would always maintain radio contact with them and either they or us would wait at one end of the pass until the vessel had cleared. This was particularly important when we were returning from James Island, as the possible results of a collision between our explosives-laden barge and another ship can be readily imagined.

The CPR business to James Island was also increasing, so they put their 18-car railcar barge TRANSFER No. 3 on the run to replace the No. 7. As soon as they had discharged her she was reloaded for Nanoose Bay, Ladysmith or as an extra to Squamish and away we would go again having only had sufficient time to refuel and pick up groceries and such, swinging our activities between the TRANSFER No. 3 and another railcar barge called the PROSPECT POINT. The routine for DOLA was so frantic at times that we had less chance of picking up the useful side jobs which filled in the gaps in her employable time.

By this time I think Dola Towing had created some envy among the bigger towboat companies because as a relative newcomer and a small operator at that, we had enjoyed great success in developing railcar barge work. With our elderly steam tug DOLA, this was unexpected by our competitors. Predatory competition has always functioned like a jungle law in the towboat business. The little guy always has the triple challenge of competing against the big fellow for the available business, raising enough capital to keep his business going without the benefit of the sophisticated sources that the big companies command, all at the same time as he keeps a constant weather eye open for the other fellow's competitive manouevres. There is no such thing as complacency in running one's business within the towboat industry if one wishes to survive.

It is little wonder that more than just a few small operators exhausted by their exertions have succumbed to the blandishments of the big competitor when he comes calling. The right time to make an approach to the little guy arises when the big fellow senses some problem, personal health, partnership strains, loss of business, loss of a vessel such as we were to suffer, or just the big fellow's predatory instincts to gobble up, coming into full play. Not unnaturally, through being a member of the B.C. Towboat Owners' Association, we had attended their meetings and we got to know most of the people in the business, including many of the people at Vancouver Tugboat Company who were to absorb my old employer, Vancouver Barge Transportation.

People at Vancouver Tug had commented that it must be pretty hard for a one vessel company to look after all the demands made upon it by customers' needs, when faced with the loss or disablement of a boat, which was perfectly true. With an operation the size of Vancouver Tug, they had a lot of flexibility and strength in their operation and could quickly provide a substitute for our boat if we were committed elsewhere. An operation like Dola had to be pretty light on its feet, and our hiring in of suitable boats was always a challenge. Vancouver Tug suggested that Dola should move in with them on a percentage basis and after discussion with my partners we went ahead with their proposal. Depending on differing perspectives, this might have been a matter of survival on our part, or it equally might have been a matter of walking into the lions's den. Time would tell!

Vancouver Tugboat Company was founded by Harry A. Jones as long ago as 1898, but when Mr. Jones died in 1919, the business became inactive, It was revived in 1924 by Harold A. Jones, the son of the founder and his sister Ruth, so like all others it had started from very small beginnings as a log tower which was

"A stately old steamer"
Pacific Great Eastern Railway's own tug the POINT ELLICE.

as far as some small companies ever went. Harold Jones, for whom I had a considerable respect, had fixed his sights on barge work, targeting the growing needs of the forest industry, and it was based on this that the company became one of the leaders in the industry.

Later, Mr. Jones told me that they were interested in buying the SALVAGE PRINCESS, a tug laying over at Pacific Drydock Company, and for sale by the Burdick interests. Harold Jones said that he understood that Dola Towing had a first right of refusal on the SALVAGE PRINCESS and did I intend to exercise it? We were not in any position to take up our option, so the proposal was that she would be purchased by Mr. Jones, his partner Art Lindsay, and chief dispatcher J.C.F. "Jim" Stewart, with a 25 per cent interest going to me, even though I did not have the money to pay for it.

I decided to take the opportunity as it seemed to offer considerable advantages, and this I suppose was the icing on the ginger cake, which came with my own and Dola's move into Vancouver Tug. I started as relief master on some of their tugs such as LA FILLE, PORT ALBERNI and LA SALLE and shortly after, an opening in the dispatch department was offered which I accepted.

I had been brought up in a school which held that the master was in charge of his vessel from the moment he left the home dock, and as such his decision was final in all matters to do with the safe operation of his vessel and the preservation of his crew. Not only did his certificate of competancy and his reputation rest on this factor, but so also did the safety of his crew, his vessel and cargo, and this has been a rule of the sea since time immemorial.

Diesel Tug CUPRITE
Owned by Steve Joyce, working with Associated.

As time went, on I became increasingly frustrated by the criticisms from my senior in the dispatch office. He insisted I was not being tough enough in pushing the masters, at times against their own better judgement, to keep going in deteriorating weather or taking tows which were at the extreme limits of both the tug's size and horsepower. It got to a stage where I could no longer condone what was expected of me in this manner, so I resigned taking the DOLA back out of their fleet and carried on as we were previously operating. As a duty dispatcher I conducted myself in a manner where I advised masters of the job to be done leaving the responsibility of how the job was undertaken and completed to them. I had always been treated in that manner myself when serving as master, in other words as a responsible professional man, rather than an inexperienced child.

I had a good chat with Mr. Jones who understood my reasons, but he made it clear that if I was leaving the "family", as he put it, I would have to sell my shares in the SALVAGE PRINCESS operation to Vancouver Tug, which was quite understandable and certainly in accord with what I would have wished to do in any event. I had no idea what they were worth when asked what I would take for them. Trustingly I told him that I would leave that up to him in determining a value and would accept whatever fair offer he cared to make. It was a good job that I had held my tongue, as when he did make his offer, the settlement was far more generous than anything I had in mind!

During my time in Vancouver Tug, I found Harold Jones and his sister Ruth to be very generous with us, offering and allowing Eunice and me with the two boys to have the use of their lovely diesel cruiser LA CAPRICE, in order to visit my parents on Saltspring Island.

There were other friends at VanTug also. Dick Tolhurst in particular became a great friend over the years and remains so to this day. Like me he had served in deepsea tramp ships and is now in retirement from Seaspan where he finished as senior vice-president. The very first time I met Dick was when the two of us and an engineer took LA GARDE out in an emergency from Vancouver Harbour to assist LA REINE which was in difficulties off Cape Roger Curtis with a railcar barge. Another friend was Rod Lindsey, son of Arthur Lindsey, who was the partner of Harold Jones. I met him during my dispatch days after he had come out of university to learn the marine transportation business. I admired and respected Rod through the years, from a trainee to his position as president of Seaspan International, in which role he passed away suddenly, still a relatively young man.

Meanwhile another important customer for Dola Towing was developing with the PGE railway which had its own tug, the POINT ELLICE, and a railcar barge, the PGE No. 2 servicing their traffic between North Vancouver and Squamish. Their business had increased so much that they needed a second fully committed barge to Squamish to supplement the POINT ELLICE and her tow.

In leaving VanTug and pursuing further business for Dola, the PGE's requirements had now increased to the point where they soon required yet a third barge, so they chartered the PROSPECT POINT from the CPR to fill in until delivery of their own new barge which was under construction. Obviously we had reached the point where the DOLA could not be in two different places at the same time, so we took the SQUAMISH QUEEN on bareboat charter to handle PGE traffic. The SQUAMISH QUEEN was a big seiner-packer type of vessel with a 400 hp heavy duty diesel in her, and she turned out to be an excellent vessel for the job, being owned by her chief engineer Art Fawcett.

When the new railcar barge PGE No. 3 came into service, business was such that a fourth tug was required. We had to do further chartering, so took the RANDY, a twin diesel type of fish-packer with two 500 hp General Motors diesels and a length of about 110 feet. She was an ex-U.S. Navy vessel owned by Tulloch-Western Fisheries Ltd. and again she proved to be a fine towboat in the service into which we placed her between North Vancouver and Squamish.

The Dola fleet had now grown to two chartered-in vessels, the SQUAMISH QUEEN and the RANDY, our own tug DOLA, plus an overseeing role for us in connection with the operation of the railway's own tug, the POINT ELLICE and its fleet of barges. Once the railway link up Howe Sound was completed in 1956, the two charters were quickly terminated, the POINT ELLICE was put up for sale by the railway and we eventually had to find other work for the DOLA.

While master of the DOLA, I was involved in two situations which are worth re-telling. The first could only be settled as it turned out through litigation, and while the event was serious enough in its consequences, the results could have been far worse with the potential loss of both DOLA and her crew.

In 1948, the American flag Liberty ship BENJAMIN H. GRIERSON was outward bound from Vancouver, heading for the First Narrows when she grounded in the shallows off the M.B. King Lumber Company mill in North Vancouver, due to a steering problem and with an ebbing tide behind her. She was unusually close inshore for this to happen and was in charge of a Canadian pilot with an American pilot on board as the ship was underway for Tacoma.

We were laying at our berth in Coal Harbour when I picked up the news that a ship had grounded, so quickly cast off to see if we could be of any assistance. When we reached the GRIERSON, we found that she was going slow ahead to hold the stern into the tide and avoid slewing around. A small tug was at her bow, so I came up to the stern and her master came down from the bridge in response to my offer of assistance. Yes, indeed the GRIERSON would like our help, so we passed our tow line aboard over her starboard quarter and he asked us to tow her up harbour, stern to, into the ebb tide.

We paid out about 400 feet of towline going from half ahead to full ahead which meant at that point we were giving her a lot of power. After some minutes of this effort she started to come astern entirely as the result of our exertions. She was not going astern on her own engine and that could be clearly seen from my vantage position at the stern controls aboard DOLA, as there was no visible propeller wash.

As soon as the GRIERSON came clear of the bottom, we manouevred her out into the main channel with the small tug assisting on her starboard forward quarter pushing her bow downstream while we now pulled her stern upstream sufficiently to clear the shallows which had caught her, and went ahead to get her back into the main ship channel for the First Narrows. We needed her to slow down sufficiently for us to be able to recover our tow line. However, without her taking sufficient way off, not enough slack was created to enable the towline to be slipped from the ship.

Aboard the GRIERSON, there was no concern for the peril she was creating for us. Roles had reversed because by now she was towing us backwards and taking everything into account the immediate danger was that we would broach and be pulled under. I tried contacting the ship on the radiophone but with no response. I tried calling the Lions Gate bridge signal station, but if they reached the GRIERSON it produced no result. I blew the international "L" on the DOLA's whistle. This was one short blast, followed by one long and two more shorts, and was the signal for "Stop, I need to communicate with you", and here again the result was just as negative.

By this time the mate had let out all 1800 feet of our tow line and it was obvious that we were going to have to sacrifice it to save further damage to the DOLA, so I told the mate to let it go after our winch had suffered some damage also.

This action saved our boat from further damage, but it certainly looked like we, as the good samaritan in this case, had been sorely abused for our efforts. We had gone to the GRIERSON's assistance with a well found boat all ready for our next assignment and came back in after a brief excursion across the harbour, minus an expensive towline, with a damaged winch and effectively a disabled tug. Replacing a towline takes some days under the best of circumstances and the winch had to be repaired to boot. I took our bill up to the ship's agents for our damages and our towing time but soon after it came back rejected by the BENJAMIN H. GRIERSON owners, with a denial that we had given any service. I took the matter up with our lawyer, Don Clark of Clark Wilson & Company, who decided that we had a good case and issued a writ against the GRIERSON owners.

The case came up in Admiralty Court before Chief Justice Sidney Smith, one of the most eminent judges in the field of marine jurisprudence. Every claim we made in setting out the truth of our position was denied, their defence being that we had not done as we were told, effectively rendering no assistance and that the ship had come off under her own power. They produced their bridge and engineroom logs to prove that they had gone astern under their own power and had thus come off under their own power. They made no suggestion as to what had happened to our missing towline in spite of the fact that it was difficult to ignore 1800 feet of one and a quarter inch steel line which was being dragged from their stern along the bottom of the harbour!

Our case was not looking too strong as the argument progressed and comparisons were made between our log and their logs. It was getting down to who was the most credible party as we produced no witnesses other than our own crew who could not have been deemed to be entirely disinterested third parties. Our counsel, Don Clark, then brought on a surprise witness who clinched the case for us. This witness proved to be the American pilot, aboard to take over as soon as the GRIERSON entered American coastal waters. He happened to be standing on the Liberty ship's lower bridge wing watching everything that went on. What the Canadian pilot was doing while all this was unfolding, I did not know. Subsequently it turned out that the Canadian pilot, Captain Flood, whom I had previously known, had died shortly after the incident. By a strange coincidence, the duty First Narrows signalman at the time of the incident, also died prior to the trial. We later had Captain Flood's widow, Mrs. Jean Flood, a wonderful lady, as cook aboard the DOLA. She treated all crew members as part of her family and referred to us all as "her boys".

When the American pilot was asked if the GRIERSON had gone astern under her own power, he was very firm in stating that if she had, he would have seen disturbed water as the ship's propeller threw up discolouration and foam which would have quickly worked its way forward to where he stood slightly ahead of amidships.

With the testimony of this witness who, with his qualifications and experience, would be judged a highly professional and disinterested witness, the case for the defendents collapsed like a house of cards, and judgement was given in our favour. As a result we recovered our damage costs, towing bill and legal costs. Justice Smith was highly critical of the falsification of the ship's logs and was satisfied that there had been collusion on board to bring this about. A ship's log at any time is a vital document which relies on honesty and accuracy for its value. Since time immemorial, it has been regarded as a legal cornerstone bearing witness to the operation of the ship and noting all the facts of the tide and weather and any other relevent detail. Tampering with it is on a par with forging a cheque or any other document.

I remember Sidney Smith remarking that it was a good job from the GRIERSON's point of view that the DOLA was a deep draft vessel. A smaller boat with less draft would have almost certainly been pulled over with the possibility of loss of life, and a very big claim for damages. In similar circumstances ships have been arrested and sold by the Admiralty marshal to meet their legal obligations, quite apart from the fact that gross negligence can also result in prison terms.

I do not know if there were any consequences for the ship's officers particularly the captain and chief engineer, who would have to take ultimate responsibility. However, I tend to the view that a great many American ships, particularly the

Liberties, were manned by wartime emergency trained crews with inadequate practical experience. In peacetime, promotion in merchant ships is generally far slower with the consequence that experience gained was absorbed more thoroughly, but during the war there was no time considering the enormous number of new ships pouring out of the yards for which crews, including officers had to be found.

The other instance became a straight insurance matter and resulted from a malfunction in the engine room aboard DOLA. In this case we were bringing the railcar barge CP No. 3 into the James Island dock where the routine required the tug to lash alongside the barge with the effect that the barge became the ship and the tug became the engines. The master would station himself on the barge, usually on the roof of a railcar, for purposes of conning her into the dock, issuing his orders from there to the tug.

I gave the order to go slow astern to take way off the barge, but she did not react as I expected. I got the correct response to each order, but she was picking up speed instead of slowing, so I called to go hard astern, but she still did not react with the result that we were now out of control. I next called for full emergency astern, and while this time the engineroom reacted as expected, it was too late as she surged ahead and crashed into the dock causing considerable damage to the float and smashing up a couple of water taxis.

When the accident was fully investigated, it turned out that a triple expansion engine might momentarily come to rest in a critical upright position when shifting from ahead to astern or vice versa. It is possible that the cams which control the reversing do not fully engage so that when the telegraph signal came from the bridge, the engineer working at his control panel, which is at deck level, has his eyes on his controls, but cannot or does not necessarily see the motion of the engine until he consciously looks to see what is happening.

The reader may regard this as being pretty careless, but should not forget that when a steam tug is involved in harbour work, such as in this instance, the orders to the engineroom for a very short period can come quite fast and heavy, and with everything depending on the engineer at the controls for a quick response, he cannot be working the controls and running around the engineroom at the same time! By today's standards, steam tugs were big and ponderous vessels, quite in contrast to the modern diesel tug with wheelhouse controls and everything at the watch officer's fingertips. There was some argument with the insurance company as to what did, and did not constitute an act of God, and what constituted negligence, but the matter was settled amicably and everyone was fully compensated.

Another incident turned out to be a mercy mission. We were on a night passage across the gulf from Nanaimo to Vancouver when the mate, Cal Himmelman, called me as he noticed a blip showing on the radar screen which we had recently installed. The blip was some seven miles away from us, and a faint flash from a light could be seen. This kept on recurring, so I decided to steer for it to investigate. When we were about three miles away, we caught sight of a brief flash from the object and eventually came alongside what turned out to be a small waterlogged open boat which had been holed following striking a deadhead. The blip we picked up was evidently the reflection from the outboard motor each time it lifted on a wave and was caught momentarily by our radar.

We got three people, two men and a girl aboard, all very much suffering from exposure after being in the water for several hours. The girl was in particularly bad shape and had only been saved by the fact that her companions had the presence of mind to tie her wrist to the boat's painter, to prevent her drifting away, which had it happened the other two would have been helpless to prevent. We managed to get them warmed up to some extent, meanwhile having called Vancouver to have an ambulance standing by when we berthed. All three were whisked into hospital suffering from hypothermia and I understand recovered, but it was provident that they had managed to keep their flashlight dry. They had seen several vessels go by, but none had noticed their light when they flashed it, so they were very fortunate that an alert mate had been curious enough to start the process of checking out their brief radar reflection.

During the eight years we had owned the DOLA, we had been very fortunate in sustaining only one stranding and one collision. The stranding occurred when the vessel went into Musgrave's Landing to pick up a tow of logs. When backing up to get a line on the tow to yard it into deeper water, DOLA had touched an outlying reef, and as the tide was falling she stranded. Being a deep draft vessel drawing about 16 feet, she fell over onto her side and quickly filled with water, spilling messy oil fuel into the harbour. Captain Jack Georgeson, our senior master, and I flew up there to see what could be done.

When we arrived we found the vessel with no crew aboard and of course all power shut down. Her stern was up in the air with the water lapping the boat deck and laying over at a severe angle on her port bilge. In the meantime I had already contacted Straits Towing and got them to send a salvage crew and equipment over to take the vessel off. I had the crew take me out to the DOLA by lifeboat. She was so far over I was able to step off the bow of the boat through the open door into the master's cabin, scrambled up to the still operable radio in the cabin, and contacted the salvage vessel which was en route.

Upon return to Vancouver, the usual marine survey was done on behalf of underwriters by Captain George Armitage of Boyd Phillips & Company, the average adjusting firm which was an arm of our brokers, Dale & Company. Among other items in an extensive inventory of repair work was the installation of a new keel, which was quite an undertaking when such long timbers were becoming increasingly difficult to find, quite apart from finding a mill capable of handling them. In spite of the extent of the damage, the underwriters found that it was still cheaper to repair her than to pay out a constructive total loss.

Days off for towboat crews under prevailing union agreements were far more reasonable for those sailing, with twenty days on duty and ten days off, which meant that I could have a master covering the twenty days, and I would relieve him for ten days, thus giving me time ashore to follow up on business contacts and hopefully benefit from new business. As crew on the DOLA I had a trusted mate and two excellent seamen who had sailed with me in the TRUCILLA. These were Gordie Willis, Walter Gordy and Colin Longmuir, and later, this put Willis up to master and Gordy up to mate.

October 28, 1953 turned out to be the last day that the DOLA ever sailed. I had been relieved at noon by Captain Jack Georgeson who took her for a routine railcar barge tow to Squamish. We had had fog for several days which was quite usual for the time of year. I had dealt with a few items of business in the afternoon and got home to be greeted by Eunice with the news that there was an emergency call from the master of the DOLA and that I should call the Vancouver marine operator right away. When I got through, the operator called the DOLA several times but got no response, and not unnaturally I was pretty worried as to what the problem might be. I figured that all being well she must have been somewhere off Whytecliff or Horseshoe Bay by now, and the thought crossed my mind that maybe she had tangled in some way in the fog with another vessel such as the Union Steamship vessel which would have been in the vicinity at the same time.

The operator tried again with no response from the DOLA, but this time another vessel came on the air. She announced that she was the LADY CYNTHIA and the voice asked if she had Captain Wilson on the line, and that the speaker was the well known Captain Billy Yates, a senior master in the Union Company.

I knew Captain Yates quite well. He said, "Ted, I'm afraid I have very bad news for you".

"Bad news! What's up Bill?" I asked.

"We had a collision in the fog, and the DOLA has gone" he replied.

"What about the crew?"

"We got them all off okay, with only one minor injury"

"Well, that's the main thing, but what about the barge", I asked.

"A tug, the BLACK BEAR 11, which was close by is hanging on to the barge and awaiting instructions", Captain Yates replied.

I got on to the recovery tug's owner and asked if she could carry on to Squamish in order to complete the tow and the owner said she could, so that looked after that worry for the time being. The DOLA was now laying in 600 feet of water between Passage Island and Whytecliffe and was clearly gone for good, but it was fortunate that the LADY CYNTHIA had been able to hold herself into the sinking vessel which slowed the ingress of water long enough to get everyone off. DOLA had been hit just abaft the boiler room, and all crew at the time of the accident were at least at main deck level with some eating a meal and no one in the foc'sle. When the LADY CYNTHIA's sharp steel stem had cut deeply into the engine room, the duty engineer was standing by the control station at main deck level. The CYNTHIA's stem touched him and knocked him aside. As she filled our crew scrambled out onto the wheelhouse and from there climbed aboard the LADY CYNTHIA.

As I have said we were fortunate in losing no crew, but losing the DOLA herself was particularly sad for me. This was our first boat and she had served the company very well. Her loss was preceded by our having made the final payment on her. At the enquiry it was determined that the LADY CYNTHIA had passed Bowyer Island in clear weather and had entered the heavy bank of fog off Whytecliffe quite suddenly, and had not immediately commenced blowing her whistle. DOLA was in the fog holding her usual course and sounding her whistle as she headed past Whytecliffe, and in another few minutes would have been out of the fog and in the clear. The LADY CYNTHIA, on entering the fog, had found herself a little closer inshore than she had figured which put her on the wrong side of our vessel in terms of the rule of the road, so she had made a slight alteration of course to starboard to adjust her position which as it turned out compounded the problem because instead of her crossing over well ahead of us, it put her on a collision course with DOLA.

Both vessels had their radar on, and the DOLA's mate on watch, Vic Montgomery, was quite happy with everything until he saw the CYNTHIA turning in to him, but by that time it was too late for DOLA with her heavy tow to take any avoiding action. The enquiry apportioned no blame to the DOLA, and we made a full recovery under our marine insurance cover.

We were now short of one tug so had to scurry around to bareboat charter a replacement and were fortunate in obtaining the LE ROI from Pacific Coyle Navigation. The LE ROI was also a steamer, rather similar to DOLA, and she filled in for us well enough until we had made more permanent arrangements. This was also the moment when Captain Murrell decided that he should retire from the company and sell his shares. He was not an old man, but felt disheartened following the loss of DOLA. His shares were picked up by the other shareholders.

Captain Harley Brown had previously sold his small tug, the DOUBLE ISLAND, and was looking for a larger replacement. Captain Brown had one in mind which he had located. This was an ex-U.S. Army tug called the PRESTIGE laying in San Diego, and he wanted me to accompany him to examine her. She was not a bad vessel, but not in a condition to bring up to Vancouver under her own power, so following his purchase of her he had the vessel towed up.

He tied her up in the north arm of the Fraser, intending over a period of time to overhaul engines and put her into a fully operative condition again. With the loss of the DOLA, we considered our replacement options and located a replacement vessel in the JOHNSTONE STRAITS ex ROBERT PRESTON, a large steam tug, first owned by Preston & Mann, which was about the last of her type to be built in 1927, and was somewhat larger than the DOLA. We negotiated an exchange with Straits Towing, with them taking the American boat, the PRESTIGE in exchange for the JOHNSTONE STRAITS with some financial adjustment, renaming her PRESTIGE ll and thus she became Harley Brown's contribution to the business.

The PRESTIGE ll was registered to the ownership of a new company, Dola Towing (1954) Ltd., following the wind-up of the original Dola Towing Ltd. and the reallocation of original shareholdings. Due to the increasing trailer traffic combined with rail cars to Vancouver Island, CPR purchased a large barge and converted it into a combined carrier which they named TRANSFER No. 4. They were also having a new combined passenger, railcar, automobile and trailer ferry built at Alexander Stephen's shipyard on the Clyde, which was to become the PRINCESS OF VANCOUVER.

In 1953 on the strength of an agreement with the CPR, our shareholders purchased the large steam tug SALVAGE CHIEFTAIN from Pacific Salvage, reverting her name to the original LILLOOET, which she bore when built. She was originally employed as a hydrographic survey vessel by the Canadian Hydrographic Service from her year of building in 1908. We registered her to a new company we set up called Pacific Towing Ltd. and were joined by two new shareholders, my brother,

Diesel Tug BEAVERMAC
Ian MacTavish's contribution to Associated Tugboats.

Captain Doug Wilson, who served in her and other Dola vessels, and Major Fred Brooks, a retired army officer.

The LILLOOET was originally tramping but later towed the railcar barge ISLAND LOGGER which was on charter from Island Tug & Barge, on a run to the CPR Nanaimo terminal where she would unload trailers following which she would proceed to Nanoose Bay rail slip to unload railcars, reload with returning railcars and then go back into Nanaimo to top off with trailers for Vancouver. This was a very tightly scheduled run due to alternating our berthing with three passenger vessels.

When the larger TRANSFER No.4 came on the scene, we were transferred to handling her. Then upon completion of the new passenger-rail slip being built in

Diesel Tug COMALONG
Owned by Bill Benson when with Associated.

Nanaimo for the PRINCESS OF VANCOUVER, it became an easier run for us with only the one stop to handle the combined cargo.

In 1956 due to later problems it was decided to scrap the LILLOOET, and Pacific Towing went into voluntary liquidation. Masters serving in the LILLOOET during her days in Pacific Towing were, Al Strang, Bert Higgs, Gordie Willis and myself. During her time with us she towed bulk cement barges from Bamberton Cement Works in Saanich Inlet to Kitimat during the construction of the aluminum smelter and townsite as required, along with our regular CPR business.

In 1954 while under command of Captain Strang, LILLOOET had an accident during dense fog when entering Vancouver Harbour. Dredgers were working in the channel and in entering the First Narrows on a flood tide with a railcar barge in tow, a bouy from the outer dredge was picked up in LILLOOET's port propeller. The vessel came to a stop with the barge glancing off her stern, cut the towline and damaged her steering. The barge struck the outer dredge, missing the inner one, and was picked up by another tug without further complications. With both steering and the port engine now out of commission the captain dropped anchor but in so doing was rammed by the inbound coastal tanker BRITAMERICAN. It was quite a mess which was left to the average adjusters and marine underwriters to sort out!

Another instance while I was master during a strong southeasterly gale, we were behind the Neck Point entrance to Nanaimo Harbour, as usual to pick up our railcar barge, the ISLAND LOGGER. The barge crew let the bridles go and the barge went by us up into the wind and I proceeded ahead to come alongside her. LILLOOET appeared to not be moving, and I found that with our draft we were on bottom. The barge with her shallower draft was now about 300 feet

LOUISE IDAHO
A hardworking boat with Associated, owned by the Towell brothers.

ahead of us and slowly coming to a stop, falling broadside to the wind, blowing across and off the flats towards Gallows Point.

With engines full astern I managed to free LILLOOET off the bottom and steamed to a position off the flats inside Gallows Point and waited for the barge to continue downwind to my position where I picked her up alongside. Anxious moments but no harm done!

I have already mentioned Dola Towing's success and the fact that as small operators we had to be on our toes constantly, ready for trouble when it arose from any one of a hundred different sources and causes, and the fact that the process creates a good deal of stress and mental fatigue. The process of living, breathing, eating and sleeping towboats is a condition which many towboat industry people will appreciate. The boat or boats are seldom out of one's mind and tend to dominate everything to the exclusion of much else which should be important in one's life. A towboat manager is something like a shepherd, always tending his flock by day and night, except that the trials and travails of towboating are not as restful as looking after sheep!

For some little time after leaving Vancouver Tug, it had been apparent to me on account of Dola's exposure to all the perils of being a small operator, that there was an opportunity to bring together a number of independent small owners under the umbrella of a management company which would function as a sort of co-operative pool.

This was an arrangement which to the best of my knowledge had never been put together before in the B.C. towboat industry, although it was not uncommon in the fishing industry and had been well and truly tested in such countries as Holland and Germany with excellent effect in operating pools of coastal freight vessels. Boats would remain under individual ownership and accounts held by one or other of the participants would be fully respected. Where it worked well was through having a full time manager/dispatcher, and a book-keeper which gave us efficient shoreside management and economies of scale in practically every function from fuelling to victualling and from manning to marine supplies. Additionally with a proper shoreside function, we would have a better chance of arranging new employment opportunities for the boats in the pool.

I contacted some of the log brokers, notably P.H. Barnett & Company and McKay & McCallum Ltd. both of whom were among the more successful in their field and knew a number of small independent tug owners. There was considerable support for the idea, so some months after having cut adrift from Vancouver Tugboat Company, we formed Associated Tugboats. In 1949 we took office space close by Menchions Shipyard and Associated was in active business. I recall that there were sceptics around the waterfront including a few among our competitors who regarded us as a "ragtag and bobtail outfit", and perhaps more of a joke than a serious threat to anyone else.

Following organisation we ended up with six members, including Dola Towing, and a total of eight tugs, with periodic charters in, when the business demanded. The participants were:-

DOLA	Dola Towing Co. Ltd.
SQUAMISH QUEEN	Dola charter
RANDY	Dola charter
COMALONG	Bill Benson
STANDFAST	Jack Gillam and Archie Thorpe
CUPRITE	Steve Joyce
LOUIS IDAHO	Towell Brothers
BEAVERMAC	Ian MacTavish

Later a ninth tug joined the group. This was the BAYBURN, owned by engineer Bill Lynd, a vessel about the size of the STANDFAST and later again we took on a tenth vessel, the DOUBLE ISLAND, owned by Harley Brown, who as described earlier, later became one of my partners in Dola Towing (1954) Ltd. This resulted in the eleventh vessel joining the fleet when PRESTIGE 11 replaced the lost DOLA. Lastly, vessel number twelve joined the fleet in the form of the previously described LILLOOET, although at that time she was still under charter from Pacific Salvage Company, and ownership was not assumed until after Dola and Associated separated.

I was elected managing director, and Harry Roberts became secretary-treasurer and office manager, with all members being directors. This was a fair arrangement with no one being able to complain about not having a proper window on what was going on in the company. All operating expenses of Associated were charged to each participating vessel equally, which dealt with office expenses and shoreside salaries, but each vessel bore its own operating expenses for its manning costs, victualling, fuel,insurance and the like.

As time went on it became more apparent that my services were needed ashore as otherwise I could not put the time in to dealing with present and future customers, not only on the mainland but also on Vancouver Island, the Gulf Islands, up coast and in the State of Washington. The business was growing to the point where additional office help was needed. Captain Ian MacTavish, owner-master of the BEAVERMAC, came ashore to take care of general vessel business and dispatching, leaving Harry Roberts free to assist me and handle complicated billing and accounting needed in an association like ours.

The three Dola boats created no problems in terms of employment as their work was steady and virtually guaranteed, but with a little hustling we were able to get enough log and scow work to keep the five smaller boats fully employed, and after a short while the members started to appreciate that it was all working out very well and certainly producing better results than anyone had experienced when working alone.

Each owner had his insurance with whomever he pleased, but with Dola Towing and our chartered boats we had always used Dale & Company as our broker and I must say that over the years I was in business this was a happy and enduring relationship. We came to know Don Black, their accounts executive, Bob Rolston, the deputy manager, and Maynard Atkinson, the average adjuster as personal friends, along with others in the Dale & Company office. Associated of course arranged all the log insurance business for flat booms in its charge and here again we dealt exclusively with Dale & Company, introducing standards of construction in the tows which gave us a far better chance of delivering them without loss. Our masters had standing orders not to pick up a tow if it did not in the master's opinion come up to standard, and then Don Black, and sometimes myself would fly up to the camp or booming ground to sort out the problem. I think our broker clients from whom we got most of our log raft business really appreciated this extra service and it paid off for Associated.

One funny incident concerned the COMALONG which was working alongside a boom in English Bay. Being a two man boat, both of the crew were on the boom with the COMALONG tied to it by a light line. A heavy swell from a passing ship caused the line to snap and away went the COMALONG under power with no one on board. This was quite a predicament and the master and his engineer mate watched the vessel take off helpless to do anything about it. As luck would have it she passed through moored yachts without touching anything, and beached herself at the seaplane slip at Jericho Beach, but by that time the two men had been picked up by a small boat and went ashore to recover their vessel. They got her off alright and with no damage done beyond feeling some embarrassment for the incident!

However, some rot started to appear in the fabric of the business. Two of the small owners had become sloppy about their responsibilities and we started to receive complaints from some of the logging companies about booms not being collected at pre-arranged times, which meant that tides and good log-towing weather might be missed along with the expense at times of having to pay for a boom man at high tide to let go the booms, and of course delays meant late deliveries. Ignoring the dispatcher's instructions created intolerable problems for the office because everything depended so much on timing, weather and tides in the towboat business if operating problems were to be minimised, but some of our members were forgetting that.

We called a director's meeting to discuss the complaints from our clients and to reiterate the obvious, which was that this type of irresponsible behaviour would damage the excellent relationship we had built up with our brokers and cause loss of business. I stated that these actions would not be tolerated and must stop immediately. At this point I was more or less told that they were not going to take orders from Harry or me. After all they were owners, perhaps forgetting that I was as well, but equally forgetting that it was mostly by Harry's and my efforts, that they enjoyed the continuation of both our services, and therefore much of their employment. I was pretty fed-up at this stage and withdrew Dola Towing and its three boats when I could see that any hope of maintaining a solid working relationship was coming to an end.

After terminating my connection with Associated in 1954, Dola opened an office in the Ford Building at Main and Hastings Street, Vancouver, from which location we continued our railcar barge business. Harry remained with Associated for a while but by 1957 it had folded and gone out of business. It proved one point at any rate. Every ship has to have a captain, and the same applies with a business. Once everyone wishes to be a chief without Indians, the writing is on the wall and it is only a matter of time before everything collapses, and that was fully proven by Associated.

Notwithstanding, the Associated Tugboats enterprise was an excellent example of the benefits of co-operation, and it worked very well so long as everyone understood and supported the agreed objectives. Towboat businesses succeed with strong leadership, an adequate flow of business, backed by sound capitalisation and competent management. We had all these elements plus a democratic concept of mutual effort which is great until beer parlour talk, and cocktail lounge chatter lead to bickering and eventual withdrawal of boats and their owners. In centrally organised companies, like Vancouver Tugboat and Island Tug & Barge, owning or controlling all their own equipment, with masters as employees, if one did not like the operation or did not fit in some way, one could leave of his own accord or be fired, and things would carry on for the company undisturbed. That was the weakness of Associated: no efficient firing mechanism existed, but be fired or leave as the case may be, and the consequences of boats leaving the co-operative fleet could be as severe as a dismemberment.

Chapter Nine

Barge Economics, Operations and Anecdotes

Modern tug and barge operations on the B.C. Coast encompass one of the most sophisticated, integrated waterborne transportation systems to be found in the world today. They cover everything from ocean going deep sea tows across the Pacific, and up and down the continental shelf from Mexico to the high Arctic, in the storm wracked waters of the west coast of Vancouver Island and the Queen Charlotte Islands, sheltered inside coastal waters, and in several river systems including the Fraser and Skeena. Local designers, shipbuilders, engineers, equipment manufacturers, and above all the tug and barge companies themselves, have been among the most innovative and forward thinking people to be found anywhere in their respective fields.

In the 57 years since I got my first job as a boy deckhand on the little DESBRISAY, whose main role was to handle the City of Victoria garbage scow, the changes in this industry have been enormous, particularly from the fifties on. The term barge was used very infrequently. The American term "float" was often applied in describing the few steel railcar barges. The commonly used word "scow" described, wood-built, flat deck vessels which took their name from the Dutch "schouw", which was probably corrupted to "scow" by the early Dutch settlers in New York and Pennsylvania, who built such vessels to transport farm produce and building materials along the rivers and streams of the eastern United States. When worn out, they probably ended up as kindling wood. Being cheap and easy to build from local lumber, such craft became common right across the continent wherever local needs demanded, and there was sufficient local timber and water to encourage their use.

In British Columbia scows were built in many places often at, or adjacent to, a local sawmill. Most commonly they were used in transporting fish to canneries, and for handling sawn lumber from mills to load alongside into sailing ships, while others brought sand and gravel into the cities such as Vancouver and Victoria as immediate local sources within city limits were exhausted. Again they were built with a view to cheapness and ease of building, but considering the heavy work they performed, their inherent strength is attested to by the fact that many had a life span of fifty years and more. Some are still around providing a solid floating foundation for houses and service buildings at coast fish farms. While they started in very small sizes, the towboat industry gradually appeared to adopt dimensions of 90' x 30' with a depth of 10' as standard, although later a beam increased to 33 feet was found to improve stability.

Early log barges were converted from iron and steel sailing ship hulls, but very few purpose-built steel scows were built prior to the second world war except for special purposes such as the carriage of railcars, where great structural strength was mandatory. This position pertained until after the second world war by which time B.C. steel shipbuilding capacity had been greatly enlarged. With the termination of wartime shipbuilding and repair work, this capacity gradually became available to the towboat industry, and by the fifties the building of steel hulled scows became increasingly commonplace.

It was at this stage that by common consent the term "scow" became reserved to the wood-built vessels just described, while the term "barge" came into widespread use in its applicability to steel-built vessels of similar design. The general practice of loading cargo on deck, rather than in the hull continued unabated, except in the carriage of oil, gasoline and liquid chemicals where it was carried in tanks within, and integral to the hull. In Europe, from which once again the "barge" originated, a barge usually stowed cargo in the hull, while a scow was commonly termed a "pontoon". This is a word which like barge might also be of Dutch origin and was adapted from military usage, when small easily transported box-like vessels were used as flotation in hastily built bridges which could be thrown across rivers, to facilitate movement by a travelling army.

The history of towboat construction in British Columbia from the earliest times to the present would fill an entire book in itself, but the second world war was to alter many concepts which might be said to have been the acceleration of entire new economic philosophies affecting towing capacities, methods pf construction, fuel and modes of propulsion, safety standards, navigation aids, manning scales and many other considerations.

The shortage and increasing obsolescence of tugs, with no new construction being permitted in B.C. yards during the war, was made up in the immediate postwar period by the availability of excellent U.S. war-built surplus vessels, several dozen having been imported into Canada and modified by B.C. towboat owners to suit their own needs. Almost all were of wood construction including a number of fine vessels of the highly successful "Mikimiki" class, which had been built on the design of a vessel of that name originating from 1929. One steel vessel from the U.S. wartime shipbuilding program found her way into a Canadian owner's fleet by a less usual route. This was the ISLAND SOVEREIGN, salvaged by Island Tug & Barge following her shipwreck in Johnstone Straits, while on passage to Alaska, and acquired by the company at that time. Island Tug rebuilt her and she became the fleet flagship, being still in service today with Seaspan International as SEASPAN SOVEREIGN.

However, these imports provided a short term answer and really nothing more, but they did provide breathing space while new policies were formulated. With the end of the war and large scale cutbacks in shipyard construction, there was a realisation on the part of the government of the day, that it was in the national interest to maintain a shipyard industry. Two factors were important in this plan. One was that escrowed tax shelter funds being held in trust for private Canadian deep sea shipowners were accumulating as such ships were disposed of to foreign owners. In theory these funds were to be used for the construction of modern postwar ships to a specification superior to the war-built ships.

Unfortunately the economics of Canadian deep sea shipping in competition with cheap foreign flags, and flags of convenience such as Liberia and Panama, plus the political realities of the day did not favour the continuation of a Canadian merchant fleet on a sufficient scale to fully utilise these funds. The peacetime merchant marine established in the flush of wartime victory just proved to be impractical in the light of all these factors, so that when these escrow funds became transferrable, considerable such money acquired at a discount, found its way into tug and barge building.

The second factor was the enactment of the Canadian Vessel Construction Assistance Act, by which a direct federal subsidy to the shipyards commencing at 40 per cent of contracted building cost, was paid to the yard upon completion of a building contract. This was designed to kick-start fresh life into shipbuilding which would have otherwise gone into rapid decline as the country buckled down to peacetime competitive conditions.

The rules did not permit an owner to take advantage of both escrow funds and the shipbuilding subsidy. The escrow funds were particularly valuable for a rebuilding or re-engineering contract, but there was yet a further factor which helped funnel investment money into the industry, this was the fast write-off provision which could be taken to cover depreciation. This was not restricted to a 100 per cent write-off over three tax years, of the amount actually invested in cash by the private owner or investor. The rule was far more generous than that, in that the write-off was taken against the contracted gross value of the vessel including the subsidy paid to the shipyard.

Assume that a barge costs $100,000 to build. The shipyard cost is reduced to a net of $60,000 as the vessel gains the shipbuilding subsidy. The investor goes to his bank and arranges a loan of $30,000 which is registered as a first ship mortgage against the new vessel. The barge has been built to meet the requirement of the first class towboat concern which needs it to meet its own contractual obligations to a major forest products company in carrying woodchips from the sawmills to the pulp mills. The owner is thus covered by a firm committment to pay him a fixed amount monthly, which he can assign to his bank in addition to the bank holding the mortgage, the whole financing package being further secured by the borrower's personal guarantee.

While the subsidy was reduced in stages until it was finally phrased out, this was a win/win scheme which suited everyone. The towboat company obtained its barge on a firm, usually five year committment without any need to invest its own funds. The forest products company obtained the services of a reliable first class vessel, at again no capital cost but at a fixed unit cost for delivery of its raw material. The shipyard had a guarantee of work and the benefits of an inflow of funds, originating from government, finance institutional and private, and the private investor had a secure, well leveraged investment and tax shelter combination. Some may say that it was a give-away program designed to help a favoured few "corporate welfare bums", but this was not so. What it was, was an incentive program which led to a large scale rebuilding, modernisation and enlargement of our towboat industry, and as an essential cog in the chain of industrial growth on the B.C. Coast everyone benefitted, including the working public dependent upon the jobs which enlarged industries provided.

The larger more progressive companies such as Island Tug, Vancouver Tugboat, Straits Towing, Rivtow Marine and Gulf of Georgia were always in touch with advantageous developments, and wasted no time in building large fleets of new steel tugs and barges. Naturally such expansion did not develop overnight; in fact it probably went on for something like twenty years. The tugs were usually financed through the towboat companies own investment resources, but the barges made an

Steam Tug LILLOOET
When owned by Pacific Towing Company and operated as part of Dola Towing's railcar towing operations.

Railcar barge ISLAND LOGGER
Showing the old style accomodation on the stern of the barge.

ideal investment for high income professional and business people. Certain accountants and law firms made something of a speciality of organising suitable individuals in a high income bracket and syndicates of investors, who would take up a given number of the 64 shares into which every registered Canadian ship is legally subdivided. Organised in this way it was possible for each investor to have direct ownership, which was mandatory, if he wished to take advantage of the depreciation and fast write-off provisions for the benefit of his personal income tax picture and thus reduce his income tax liability arising from all his sources of income.

The flexibility of welded steel shipbuilding techniques were well understood and opened up an enormous field for improved design concepts, far larger barges and more powerful and economical tugs. These trends made the remaining steam tugs such as our PRESTIGE 11 more or less obsolete overnight, unless alert owners had dieselised otherwise good servicable vessels ahead of time before the incentives which favoured new construction really got under way during the fifties. The process of obsolescence was accelerated even more quickly by rapidly changing technology such as bridge controlled enginerooms, new navigation aids and kort nozzles which improved propeller efficiency and steering. Long overdue crew needs received greater attention both in terms of safety and comfort, but most importantly to vessel operating economics, greater vessel efficiency allowed smaller crews, handling more compact and powerful vessels which were capable of delivering bigger tows of both log booms, and barges anywhere along the coast.

It is difficult to theorise on whether the greatest changes took place in tugs or barges. Probably the changes in each type of vessel ran concurrently with each other, but by the mid-fifties the process of building wood scows was virtually dead. Mercer Brothers Star Shipyards at New Westminster were probably the last builders of such vessels, while another well-known barge builder, Mackenzie Barge & Derrick Company at Dollarton, North Vancouver are believed to have built their last wood barge in the early fifties, but these yards like others of consequence moved into steel boat and barge building.

Steel construction, as previously noted, permitted the design and building of barges of a hitherto undreamed size and capacity. The standard 90' x 30' wood scow of yesteryear immediately jumped to a length of 120' in the new steel barges, and from then on sizes increased so that a 200' plus barge, lifting 5000 tons of aggregates or other cargo is now quite commonplace.

The old hog fuel scows, were simply flatdecks with a rudimentary box erected on deck to contain the wood waste with which they were loaded. This material was transported from sawmills to pulp mills to burn as fuel under the steam boilers. Barge sizes increased rapidly as hog fuel gave way to vaster tonnages of wood chips an even more important sawmill byproduct for which the pulp mills had an insatiable appetite. Wood chips are a valuable commodity which nowadays go far afield as an export to Japan and South Korea, and much of the hog fuel consumption has been replaced by bunker oil as a source of energy, and that in turn is giving way to natural gas as it becames available.

The most dramatic size increase was in the self-loading, self-dumping log barges, which replaced the old sailing ship hulls with a deadweight capacity seldom exceeding 3,000 tons, and the big Davis rafts. When the ISLAND FORESTER, later

"Riding the Rails"
The master's view from the roof of a box car while berthing PGE No. 2 at Squamish.
Tug SQUAMISH QUEEN alongside.

SEASPAN FORESTER, was built, she reached the largest size ever attained in a B.C. coast barge with a deadweight capacity of some 20,000 tons.

Some of the most sophisticated equipment was to be found in chemical and petroleum product barges. These covered a wide range of sizes and capability according to the needs of the trade in which they were employed. Roll-on, roll-off barges, equipped with vehicular ramps revolutionised the transport of much vehicle traffic, including the ability to quickly load and offload logging equipment at remote beaches.

Efficient tug and barge operations aim to give the customer faster, more efficient and safer service at a competitive cost. The function of all companies in the industry is to operate within the framework of a formula by which a ton of cargo can be moved by the lowest feasible horesepower, in the shortest possible time. That is what towboat economics are all about and while many other factors have a bearing, such as the cost and consumption of fuel, marine insurance and manning costs, the reader will appreciate as in any other form of transportation, this is the reason why carrying capacities of barges have climbed so drastically and horsepowers of tugs have increased proportionately as operators seek economies of scale. A whole host of operating efficiencies have grown out of all recognition to the position which pertained when the author went into the industry.

Vessel design sometimes created handling problems for towboat masters. All barges are a compromise of sorts, and those with ship shaped bows for example are usually built to better handle the hazards of deep sea tows, while the barges of rectangular form are most favoured on shorter hauls along the coast itself. The rectangular barge, from a towboat master's point of view, may have been easier to handle in almost all situations where the barge had to be wrestled in and out of berths, because each corner gives the towboat more flexibility in moving the barge around.

I found in CP's TRANSFER NO.3 and TRANSFER NO. 4, that in these two stern loaders with their ship shaped bows, they were an asset in getting alongside them for a landing. The bow is brought up on the towline to whichever stern quarter of the tug the master wishes to place her. A deckhand went off our stern up the bow ladder to the main deck to receive our spring line. In the meantime we were backing up against the barge quarter, and with her way on we pivoted and came together. Playing the towline accordingly we moved up to the deckhand's position, handed him the fixed spring line. When it came tight, we went hard over on the helm to bring the bow in. Then we handed him the wire fixed head line and manila preventer, came hard over again in the opposite direction to take up the fixed line and brought the towline tight to secure the tug alongside fore and aft.

The average pick-up time, from time of the deckhand getting on the ladder, to being secured and underway was two minutes with the barge never being off the line. In departing we would back out of the slip, let go lines, then swing on our tow and be on our way. In the event of a towline landing at a slip there was a need to have an assist tug on the barge stern.

In the case of rectangular railcar barges, which could handle cars only over the bow, to take it alongside one had to bring her up to the stern, get a deckhand on board to let go both bridles, then back away and come back placing the tug alongside the barge with the barge drifting free. This handling problem did not exist in the days when crews were carried on the railcar barges, as a master could shorten up at half speed, have a seaman let go bridles as signalled by the towboat whistle, heave in your towline on deck, then catch up to the barge that had been steered past, and held on a steady course.

Scows or barges that could be landed on the towline without any problem in unloading were easy, as one did not have to bring the scow or barge alongside the tug. One thing in favour of the rectangular railcar barges became apparent when departing from a slip in a gale. This was that the tug backed in stern first under the rake of the barge and secured bridles, so that in departing all was set for paying out on the towline. Under similar conditions with a ship-shaped bow type railcar barge, one had to back the tug up to the barge bow and pick up the pennant for securing to the towline. Once secured, upon a whistle signal, shore crew would let the lines go from the slipway and the slip and we were then on our way.

Of all the barge types which I have towed, I believe that my longest association has been with the railcar barges. Dola Towing was started with a CPR contract towing small railcar barges between Vancouver and James Island. During the eleven years of our existance railcar barge towing for the Canadian Pacific and Pacific Great Eastern railways was the most important source of employment for our own boats and the several we chartered, we were fortunate in never causing a serious accident which brought about large scale disruption to the railway system, but given the conditions under which we sometimes operated, it would have been easy enough to have something very unfortunate happen.

"Nearly Gone, but stopped in time"
A railcar caught over the end of the barge.

The CPR system was not quite so vulnerable as they had two ramps in Vancouver harbour. The older ramp, known as the east slip, was steeper at extremes of the tide which tended to reduce its effectiveness. The newer and larger west slip was to be preferred as it was not as steep, but two ramps provided insurance in case one was knocked out or undergoing heavy maintenance.

Also for many years, traffic went into both Ladysmith and Nanoose Bay, so here again if one ramp was knocked out, the system had an alternative in the event of one or other being out of commission, even if the result also meant a great deal more hauling over the tracks. With the PGE, loading at Vancouver was done over the CP slips, but no such alternative existed at Squamish, which made the entire system highly vulnerable if the Squamish slip was knocked out.

Popular humour of the day used to describe the PGE as the "Please Go Easy", or the railway which started nowhere and ended nowhere. It had no alternative connection with any other railway until the two extensions from Quesnel to Prince George, and the connection down Howe Sound from Squamish to North Vancouver were built. The PGE of the forties and early fifties was a pretty rickety affair with a lot of old equipment and very light track, quite unlike the first class railroad it has since become.

Squamish in winter was no picnic and a winter tow in a driving Squamish wind with blinding snow and a heavy wind chill factor created special hazards. On many occasions we arrived at Squamish so badly coated in frozen spray, freezing rain or just plain snow, that we almost looked like we had been navigating the high Arctic. Often the cars were frozen to the rails with couplers and car brakes equally frozen. The steam available aboard DOLA and her successor PRESTIGE ll came in

"Frozen to the rails"
Railcars coated with ice. Steam was used to clear the ice.

"This one was less lucky"
This car went overside and is floating on air trapped inside, as it awaits a lift out of the water.

Steam tug PRESTIGE II docking a railcar barge at Squamish.

Steam Tug PRESTIGE II
Which was acquired by Dola Towing to replace the DOLA following her loss. Outward bound through the Lion's Gate, towing the ISLAND LOGGER now minus her crew accomodation.

very handy. The diesel-propelled vessels were not quite so convenient in this regard, as they had to rely on shore generated steam for de-icing purposes.

To bring the barge into the Squamish slip as in any other, required the towboat master to con his tow in by climbing onto a well placed boxcar, from which vantage point he could see the slip and give directions to the mate aboard the tug, who was otherwise blind, being obscured alongside the loaded railcar barge, with the high cars between him and the slip blocking his vision. Being on the roof of an ice covered boxcar was a hazard in itself, but when berthing in a heavy snowstorm with a severe wind chill or in blinding rain, for both of which Squamish was notorious, the entire routine of berthing put everyone concerned on his metal.

Chilled to the bone, with even one's eye moisture seeming to freeze, and with ice forming on the lashes, lips and nostrils was an unpleasant experience which I quickly learned was best controlled with a generous smear of vaseline before even venturing outside the wheelhouse. In spite of the discomfort which had to be endured, it did not really matter what the conditions were. The tug and barge were a part of the railway schedule and at all costs the traffic had to go through to avoid scheduling bottlenecks. Aside from the precision with which the two vessels had to be handled, it will be equally obvious that the master and the mate had to function as one, and that a skilled crew was a decided asset.

Probably the most common form of accident was not with the barge, but with the railcars. Once safely berthed the towboat crew could relax as everything now became the responsibility of the railway crew. A malfunction or carelessness occasionally saw a car fall between the ramp and the barge itself, or derail. Another version of a car mishap could arise when a car became uncoupled and ran down the ramp, tearing the end stops out and going over the barge stern into the water. Such accidents were awkward but seldom fatal, and some delay would be inevitable until lifting gear arrived to put the car back on the track. When they went over the stern, these cars were more difficult to salvage, but unless they were in our way, they could be left to the railway to deal with after we had left the berth.

We had known for sometime that the PGE was building extensions from both existing ends of the railway and when completed it would mean the end of our barge service into Squamish. The rail connection between Squamish and North Vancouver was opened in 1956 and our prospects changed overnight. We returned the chartered vessels RANDY and SQUAMISH QUEEN to their owners and looked around for suitable employment for PRESTIGE 11. Harold Elworthy of Island Tug & Barge took the vessel on an agreed day rate charter.

This charter lasted about a year during which time we continued to handle railcar barges for Island Tug, which controlled a big proportion of the available traffic, including dangerous cargo into Victoria and a regular barge run from Victoria down to Seattle and Tacoma, and from those points back to Vancouver, on what amounted to a triangular run. These longer trips involved a different routine to the essentially short hauls I was used to, in going to Squamish and central Vancouver Island points. They also further underlined the great importance of the various routings across the Straits of Georgia and Puget Sound, in extending the two Canadian transcontinental railways and at least three parallel American lines to the south.

Diesel Tug SEA LION
Probably the author's favourite vessel of all he served aboard. A former steam tug and the possessor of the famous musical whistle.

The Canadian Pacific, and Canadian National require little explanation beyond noting that they each had smaller systems of their own on Vancouver Island which each gathered quite a lot of contiguous mill and general freight traffic, the three American railways were the Great Northern (GN), the Northern Pacific (NP) which was controlled by GN, and the Chicago, Milwaukee, St. Paul and Pacific, popularly known as the "Milwaukee Road".

Both GN and NP combined with the third GN controlled railway, the Chicago, Burlington & Quincy, in a huge railroad merger which became the Burlington Northern system of today. The Milwaukee eventually went bankrupt and its system was broken into a number of smaller railways. The Island Tug & Barge service to and from Puget Sound enabled the American railroads to more economically get their traffic directly to and from the sources of freight, and thus bypass expensive time consuming interchanging through Vancouver, usually involving two of four Canadian lines.

A good example of this bypass was the movement in and out of Squamish of American traffic directly down to Puget Sound which continued for some years after the North Vancouver connection was made. Had this service not been available, lumber cars bound from say Quesnel, for a destination on the Milwaukee would have to interchange over the CN, and from that system pass over the B.C. Hydro Railway, Great Northern or Northern Pacific to get on to the Milwaukee. By interchanging in this way a freight bill for a carload of lumber would be split between up to four different railroads. The barge run reduced this to a split between two railroads, which illustrates the advantage which might apply on a combined rail and water route.

During the year that we were on charter to Island Tug, it became increasingly obvious that costs were working against the viability of small one vessel steam tow-boat companies. We knew that the charter to Island Tug could only continue so long as it was profitable for both them and ourselves, but with new union agreements governing guaranteed time off, better working conditions and rates of pay, our boat with a crew of ten was clearly following the dinosaurs to extinction. New steel diesel boats with twice or three times our horsepower and a crew of four or five were now coming into service, and any thought on our part of dieselising PRESTIGE 11, even though physically feasible, was simply out of the question financially. A few years earlier she would have made a fine candidate for diesel conversion as she was very sound and fully on a par with others which had been converted.

As we did not have the resources available to us without a massive bank loan to cover the conversion, and even though our bankers, the Royal Bank, were willing to provide funding for this purpose, we decided against it as we still would have had a thirty year-old wood hull to work with. We offered the vessel to both Island Tug and Vancouver Tugboat but neither were now interested as they had new ultra-modern steel vessels coming along. The shareholders of Dola Towing (1954) Ltd. decided to wind up the company in 1957, so we settled all our outstanding obligations and folded the tent. We had made a good living out of it, and a lot of payroll dollars had been generated over the years to our crews.

Harold Elworthy immediately engaged our entire crew, and offered me command of the SEA LION, herself a successful diesel conversion from a steam tug. He knew that we had been a successful operation, and all our people were highly experiened in railcar barging.

I thus became a salaried master again for Island Tug & Barge, and could now concentrate on the one job of running a tug and barge while others worried about cash flow, meeting committments and drumming up new business, and this will be the subject of the next chapter.

Chapter Ten

Service With Island Tug & Barge Ltd.

As I have noted SEA LION was a former steamer and in making the conversion to diesel, no expense had been spared to commission a first class vessel. The crew accomodation throughout including my own quarters were very good in every way. Equipped with an 800 h.p. Enterprise diesel, she was placed on the run from Vancouver to Nanaimo hauling the Canadian Pacific railcar barge TRANSFER No. 4 in a scheduled service integrated into the schedules of the C.P. passenger and railcar ferry PRINCESS OF VANCOUVER. We did one round trip per day including all the dangerous cargo, to the three done by the PRINCESS OF VANCOUVER. To avoid any bottlenecks at either terminal required close cooperation between the SEA LION and PRINCESS OF VANCOUVER. The SEA LION incidentally, still retained her famous musical whistle which never failed to excite attention when coming through the first Narrows, blowing a tune. The whistle was now powered by compressed air as the vessel no longer had steam available. The novelty used to excite a lot of attention from the public, and passengers on the cruise liners, for whom, whenever possible we put on a bit of show.

The commencement of P & O cruise liner service to Alaska gave the SEA LION a chance to perform with her unusual musical whistle as her schedule always made her available to assist the Cates tugs in docking the liners at the CPR terminal.

We would meet a liner outside the First Narrows to escort her past Brockton Point and into her berth. I had practiced two tunes on the musical whistle which were "Now is the Hour" and "How dry I Am", and upon approaching an incoming liner we greeted them with these tunes, much to the delight of her passengers and CPR guests aboard SEA LION. The famous musical whistle would sound its notes right across the harbour and a good part of the city, particularly the north shore where the mountains caught the echo perfectly. My co-author tells me that when working in his garden in West Vancouver, his then young children would hear the tuneful whistle, and would become excited because they thought the icecream vendor was coming around the neighbourhood!

When I first came on this service the routine commenced with loading at Vancouver, which in itself was a time consuming process. Then the mate would take the watch over to Nanaimo, where we would unload and reload for the return trip, with me taking the watch back to Vancouver. We found that the routine became exhausting with inadequate sleep, so I took it up with the company who were very reasonable about it, and saw my point. They gave us an unlicensed second mate to take the watch on one trip with the mate taking the other. This relieved me from keeping either watch so that I was free to look after docking, loading and reloading routines and undocking. The extra man took some of the stress out of the job for all of us, and enabled the mate and particularly myself to get a decent rest.

A crew, particularly key members like the master and mate, do not perform at their best when unnecessary stress is introduced by inadequate rest. This was particularly important on this route, considering the traffic situation with which we were faced, and this was doubly so when entering and leaving Vancouver harbour. Periodically the routine was broken by small boat incidents, such as being out of gas or suffering some engine trouble or events involving other tugs. Some of these incidents had all the potential to be serious with lives at stake and I will now recount a few.

I remember one particular instance when quite a southeaster was blowing. We came alongside a 30 foot pleasure boat which had engine trouble. I was reluctant to put the engineer aboard because of the sea that was running, and after some consultation back and forth, it appeared that there was probably little we could do for them in any event. I did not think it was wise to leave them and we could not afford to take the time to wait until a rescue craft came up so decided to take them aboard, while our crew managed to move the boat to the stern of our barge, to which we tied her for the balance of the trip into Vancouver.

Two men and two women came aboard, and it was evident that there had been considerable drinking. The most important thing they seemed to believe they had, was a kit bag full of what turned out to have more booze in it. I told them they were not bringing that stuff on board, so I was challenged as to what they should do with it. I told them I did not care what they did with it, but if they tried to bring it aboard I would return them to their own boat, and they had better make up their minds quickly as we were wasting time hove to. They dumped the whole lot into the water and preferred to be aboard SEA LION rather than be left to their own devices. There was no further incident, and when we reached English Bay, we radioed for assistance for them and from then on left them in charge of a rescue boat.

We saw an awful lot of evidence of heavy drinking on the water, with boats in charge of people who would have been locked up if they had been found on the road in such a state. I think a lot of people assume that a boat in charge of a drunken person is only a slight hazard compared to a vehicle on the road, and while the chance of collision is far less it is true, the danger on boats is the lack of good judgement that follows a whole host of possible events, such as fire, when a cool head and the ability to take sensible precautions may be the only thing between safety and disaster.

Another rescue operation we undertook could have had big consequences. We were approaching Snake Island with a loaded railcar barge when we picked up a message from Airsea Rescue Coordination in Vancouver. Apparently the Straits tug BURNABY STRAITS was heading west with two loaded chip barges when she lost power in the vicinity of Thrasher Rock and was barely able to hold her own against severe sea conditions. We responded, after checking with the C.P.R. who were agreeable to us tying up our barge and going to the stricken tug's rescue. When we reached her she was in danger of going back onto the Thrasher. The mate fired the line gun and our light line was grabbed without a hitch so that our tow line could be pulled aboard. Unfortunately the deckhand aboard the BURNABY STRAITS in trying to do things properly by passing it through the port forward fairlead, accidently let the tow line go, and we were back to square one.

The wind at this time was gusting 35-45 mph with a very heavy sea running. In turning to make a second approach on the BURNABY's port side, we took aboard a starboard forward quarter sea. This engulfed the whole lower deck and had me, standing as I was, at the boat deck helm and controls, in water up to my waist. Fortunately at this point our mate and deck hands were under the break of the aft housework or they would have been washed overboard.

This time I told my mate that I would come very close to the BURNABY STRAITS. I suggested to her master that this time our line should just be placed over the bollard without coming through the port, for just as long as it would take to move them out of immediate danger. The episode ended successfully with the BURNABY and her two barges now towed to safety. Whatever the problem in her engineroom, it was quickly dealt with by the owners who had her towing chip barges again within a short while. The next time we saw her she got on the radiophone and said, "From the BURNABY STRAITS to SEA LION. We wish to express our gratitude to all aboard from all of us". It was a good example of the brotherhood of the sea.

Occasionally while on the Nanaimo run, we found that we had a stowaway on board the barge. Some of the cars were loaded with liquor for the Liquor Control Board, while others had high value merchandise consigned to one or other of the major store chains. The CPR police of course were alert for this and were watchful for cars with broken seals and any broaching of the cargo as this created an automatic claim against the railway.

One incident left a red face, but nothing beyond that. We had left the dock at Vancouver with a full load and I gave our usual whistle warning signal in good time and away we went. Now, at one time these barges carried a small barge crew of three who were accomodated in an island bridge where they could see the entire barge and the towboat ahead. These crews had been dispensed with but the accomodation still remained. When we were about two hours off Snake Island near the entrance to Nanaimo harbour, the mate thought he saw something odd on the barge, which of course was located a fair distance astern. He thought he could see a light in the accomodation wheelhouse, but given the state of the weather there was nothing we could do about it and just assumed that we had another stowaway on board. When we arrived at Nanaimo, we found that there was indeed an involuntary stowaway who was a C.P.R. policeman!

He had been checking cars following loading at Vancouver and had not heard my departure signal. In any event we took him on board for the return trip and radioed that we did have a stowaway aboard, but by this time several hours had elapsed since he had gone off duty and the alarm had gone out to find him. The first thing that always happens when anyone works around the waterfront is to assume that the missing person might have fallen in the water and drowned. However, with his discovery the alarm was cancelled with considerable relief, although no doubt when he got back he took some kidding from his colleagues.

Our chief engineer was a man who enjoyed cooking as a hobby. When I got up at about 3 a.m. to dock the vessel at Nanaimo, he invariably had a large bowl of steaming soup ready, which was good to have before going out to brave the elements preparatory to docking. He found out that I liked tripe and onions for which he, being an Englishman, had a particular fondness. Every so often as a treat for both of us, he would cook up a mess of this delicacy. The night shift of the R.C.M.P. used to drop down to see us and would usually enjoy a cup of coffee on

m.v. ELDOMA
An early unit in the Island Tug & Barge fleet.

Steam Tug "Swell"
A veteran of the Victoria Tugboat Company fleet, which was taken over by Island Tug & Barge Ltd. in 1959. This grand old steamer provided a working berth for the author during school holidays.

board, until one occasion when the duty constable came aboard and saw us tucking into our tripe and onions. "Tripe and Onions!" he exclaimed enthusiastically, so we gave him a bowl of something he had not tasted for a long time. He was also an Englishman, formerly in the Royal Navy Fleet Air Arm and whenever we had tripe and onions he would have a nose for the stuff and came aboard. We became very good friends as a result and when we moved our home to Deep Cove, North Vancouver some years later, we found that he had been transferred there as officer-in-charge of the local area detachment and the friendship continues right up to the present day.

One incident I remember very well with dangerous cargo, could have lead to a nasty explosion and fire. As I went to my docking station on the barge, I noticed that something was amiss with one of our tank trailers. On checking, it turned out that the tank had sprung a leak, and propane which was carried under pressure, was hissing out leaving a white icing all around the leak and down on the deck of the barge. This was a situation calling for great caution as we docked, as liquid propane freed of pressure spread an unseen, but highly volatile explosive cloud before it was able to disperse. We had a highway tractor from the propane company waiting when we arrived but there was no way that the driver could do anything about it. We had already called the City of Nanaimo fire department who arrived to take care of the situation.

Another more common incident involving trailers was when the parking legs of the trailer collapsed so that the trailer landed on its nose. This type of accident was more of an inconvenience than anything, and when it happened it caused delay, until a crane truck arrived to lift the damaged unit onto a tractor for removal. That was one reason why we had to be careful about our choice of courses in order to make the easiest ride for both the barge and the cargo. While everything was secured and wheel blocked with air brakes locked, some motion was unavoidable with the bulk of the weight in a loaded trailer being high up. If the barge is rolling and pitching severely, it puts a tremendous strain on the trailer parking legs, which are built to take the vertical compression strain created by the weight of the trailer, but do not permit excessive swinging from side to side, which would be the most likely cause of failure.

Continuous fog was another major hazard we frequently had to contend with on this run. I think in those days it was far worse than anything we have to contend with today. One can certainly appreciate that the cleaner atmosphere we now have with little or no burning of coal, plus the fact that sawmill beehive burners are now few and far between, has helped a great deal in reducing fog conditions, and radar has been the biggest blessing ever invented for navigating one's way through it. On many an occasion we would leave Vancouver harbour in heavy fog and then seemingly sail in a cloud until we reached the slip at Nanaimo. I remember one lengthy period when we did fourteen days sea duty with thirteen of them depending solely on radar, fog horns and whistle echoes. On only one of those fourteen days did we have reasonable visibility. Some people find fog pretty unnerving and claustrophobic; in fact my mate on this stint had to be taken off and relieved after seven days, handing over to a relief mate.

Talking about fog, I remember one evening when Eunice and I were invited for a social gathering at the Canadian Pacific marine superintendent's house, and he was talking to a few people about the fog, saying that the PRINCESS OF VANCOUVER was apparently the longest vessel that had come through the Lions Gate during the last several days. I saw the opportunity for a bit of a legpull, so I said to Captain Gillison.

"Pardon me Captain, you have just said that the PRINCESS OF VANCOUVER is the longest vessel to have come through the Lions Gate during this fog spell"

"That's right" said the Captain.

"Well I think you are wrong Captain, because the SEA LION is the longest. The SEA LION herself is 120 feet long and then we have 300 feet of towline out, followed by a barge measuring over 200 feet, and that's a lot longer than the PRINCESS, and better than that, we kept our schedule all along, did'nt we?"

He laughed. "By gosh Ted, your right".

During my time with Island Tug on the Nanaimo run SEA LION was replaced on occasion by the ISLAND CHALLENGER, another wood tug, with a length of 90 feet built during the war for the U.S. Army Transportation Service and powered by a 765 hp Caterpiller diesel. The other boat which substituted was the quite new steelbuilt, twin screw ISLAND MARINER powered by two 600 h.p. diesels. One incident which occurred involved the only stranding I had in the twelve years I had afloat with Island Tug.

On this occasion I had the ISLAND CHALLENGER and as was our usual custom the mate took over once we had cleared Vancouver harbour, calling me when we were midway between Entrance Island outside Nanaimo and the Snake Island buoy. I felt a jolt to be followed by the mate calling me to say we had gone ashore. I went up on the bridge in my shorts to see what had happened. The boat had of course stopped, but the barge was steadily riding up towards us, as if to overrun us. Two of the crew said it was time to jump overboard, but I cautioned them to wait as I believed that as the barge got closer, the dip of the tow line would rapidly increase and should hang up on the bottom thus bringing the barge to a stop. As it turned out this was exactly what happened, and our two crewmen avoided a dunking and a possible drowning. The command to "abandon ship" was unnecessary, so it was a good job they were not permitted to take affairs into their own hands.

We had hit Gabriola Island, with the tug herself riding over a ridge into what was really a deep water pool. I radioed to Island Tug who sent out a salvage boat. The vessel was lightened by removing all the fuel and water on board. Then two empty scows were placed on either side of ISLAND CHALLENGER at low water and the vessel securely lashed fore and aft to them. As the tide came up, the vessel was lightened even more by the scows taking her weight, and eventually at high water, all three were moved out of the natural basin and over the reef into deep water with little damage other than some minor scrapes to her bottom along the keel. Fortunately there were no weather problems to complicate the issue as, had a westerly come up, we would have been in very serious trouble.

At the enquiry which followed, it was determined that the mate who was taking pills for a medical reason, had collapsed in the wheelhouse for just long enough for matters to get out of hand. I thought at first that he might have fallen asleep at the wheel, which was not unknown and undoubtedly had caused many marine accidents. The company wanted to let him go but when asked, I said that there were

Diesel Tug ISLAND NAVIGATOR (2)
One of the larger units of the Island Tug & Barge fleet, prior to the Seaspan merger
fleet standing by the railcar barge PROSPECT POINT.

mitigating circumstances and he should be given another chance as he had never given me any reason for concern. In fact he had a deepsea master's ticket and lots of experience. However, they demoted him to deckhand for six months and then brought him back up to mate, and so far as I know he never had any further problem.

When I had the ISLAND CHALLENGER, I was put on a different run, this time to take two paper barges up to Port Alice on the northwest coast of Vancouver Island. Being winter we were not allowed to undertake a tandem tow around Cape Scott, so left one barge at Port Hardy, taking the other around to Port Alice and then returning light. We then went through the same routine in reverse, putting together a tandem tow of the two loaded barges from Port Hardy to Vancouver.

The weather can be terrible around the north end of Vancouver Island. In fact I always called it Cape Horn even though I had never experienced that fearsome cape. We had left Port Alice in relatively fine weather with a light northwester, and it looked like we were in for an easy ride. However anyone navigating that part of the world always kept their ear tuned to Bull Harbour radio for weather information, which continued to predict fine weather. When the mate took over the watch the seas came up accompanied with heavy snow and a high wind. By the time we reached Cape Scott the seas were so bad that we did a quarter course change towards Cape Caution in order to put the sea behind us, as it was blowing more from the west than the northwest. I called Bull Harbour and asked if there had been any change in the weather forecast. The radio operator stated "no change" until I told him what we were going through at which time he put out a warning to all shipping. Such is the changeability of coast weather and the ease with which one can be taken unawares by a treacherous change in conditions.

When we arrived at the C.N.R. dock in Vancouver with our two loaded paper barges, the longshoremen could not open the doors of the second one which was the one we were caught with in the bad weather just described. This created a real problem and much delay until the problem had been solved. What of course had happened, was that the large rolls of paper had been disturbed in the bad weather and rolled against the doors. This was also the first time I met our manager of bulk cargo, Harold Crompton, a well known figure in the towboat industry.

On another occasion in the ISLAND CHALLENGER, while going around Cape Scott, I had been turned in for some time when I felt the ship shuddering and pitching heavily. I went up to the wheelhouse to find out what was happening, and found the mate enjoying himself hugely as he drove the vessel at full power into the waves taking solid water on board.

I was pretty angry, "What are you trying to do, drown us all and break the ship up as well?"

He got her down to half speed right away, as I told him never to try that again. Once a vessel starts shipping green water, one does not fool around with nature. He slows the ship down and gives her a chance to clear herself of solid water, otherwise running the risk of burying her right under. Large ships have been lost in this manner as under the press of thousands of tons of water, hatches can be stove in, and structural failure may well follow if the ship cannot clear herself of the weight quickly enough.

The reader will recall my recounting the incident aboard the CITY OF VANCOUVER years ago, when solid water inundated the ship and plucked the mate off the bridge to what in this instance was fortunately not his certain fate. By the slenderest of chances, he was redeposited by the same wave onto the after welldeck of the ship. Wave power was also again demonstrated aboard the CITY OF VANCOUVER, a far larger vessel than ISLAND CHALLENGER, when a huge sea removed most of the forward deck cargo, brought down the foremast and came close to causing the loss of the ship.

Island Tug developed the socalled "grub run" around northern Vancouver Island, but it was not until some time later that I was transferred to that service. In the meantime ISLAND CHALLENGER was put onto a shorter version of this service, towing a covered freight barge up to Telegraph Harbour, Beavercove, Port McNeill, Alert Bay, Sointula and Port Hardy. However, for me this did not last long as I returned to my old vessel, the SEA LION, which was now towing a specialised chemical barge, called the ISLAND PINE up to Prince Rupert to service the Columbia Cellulose mill. For this purpose she carried liquid caustic soda in tanks below deck, and had three big tanks welded to her cargo deck in which she carried chlorine.

We operated a tight schedule, involving a ten day round trip. Sometimes we alternated, loading in Tacoma, and returning to North Vancouver, and vice versa. On our current work routine of twenty days on, and ten days off, this worked out quite nicely, giving two full round trips during each period on duty.

The obligations involved on this trip were considerable. The schedule, given the distance involved, was quite tight with little room for delay due to fog or any other eventuality. The nature of the cargo itself was such that everyone involved had to always be mindful of the hazards and the potential for injury and death in the event of any mishandling or mistakes. So far as the trip north was concerned with loaded cargo, extra vigilance was required in relation to other shipping. In fact we used to put out frequent radio warnings, stating our position and speed for the benefit of any passing shipping. The Inside Passage was then, as it is today, an important traffic artery for all types of shipping including a variety of Alaska bound cruise liners. Oncoming shipping in particular treated us with great caution, but we would maintain radio contact and agree with each other, that either they or ourselves would slow down and wait for the other when entering narrow passes or blind turns around points or headlands.

Proper scheduling was very important from the mill's point of view, so our practice was to give them notification by radio at 24 hours and then 12 hours prior to arrival, followed by a final warning as we reached the top end of Grenville Channel and when about three hours out. This was necessary in case we needed a standby assist tug and so that all arrangements for discharge were ready upon arrival, because no matter what the time of day, once we were secured alongside, it became the mill's responsibility to attend to discharge of cargo. Any delay caused by the mill ended up by their incurring demurrage charges as is usual in contracts of affreightment or charters. Canada Customs would become most upset if their officer was unduly delayed or held up, if our load was ex-Tacoma.

The routine which followed required us to first discharge the caustic soda at a dock a little beyond the mill. After that was pumped off, we moved back to the main mill dock to discharge the chlorine. Strict no smoking rules applied and watches continued with the tug usually tied at the aft end of the barge with the towline rigged and ready to go. One bad incident I remember occurred when we were unloading chlorine while the mate and his deckhand were on watch. I had turned in when the mate knocked and said "Cap, I think you had better come up on the dock. It looks like we have a problem".

There was a falling tide and it was about 3 a.m.. I got dressed and noticed, without the mate having to say it, that the chlorine discharge hose was stretched tight, so much so that it might have broken thus creating a dangerous chlorine spill. The mate had all ready been up to warn the dockman that the hose was being stretched as the vessel fell on the tide. Now pumping off, and all discharge gear including this line, was the responsibility of the mill, and for this purpose they stationed a pumpman to tend to everything. We never touched anything to do with this process, so I went into the hut where the pumpman was located and found that he had passed out. The cause was not hard to detect as he reeked of liquor, and there was an empty gin bottle lying on the floor. I called the mill who treated the situation as an emergency, which it was, and sent down adequate help to turn off the pump, and pay out the hose.

On another occasion, I went up on the caustic dock and caught a strong smell of chlorine gas. It is deadly stuff so I beat a very quick retreat back on board. An alarm had been sounded but we had not heard it. Until matters got back to normal we moved SEA LION off into the stream as a safety measure.

As usual fog was a particular hazard on this route which would have been inoperable with our type of cargo, without the benefit of radar. The worst instance I ever experienced, saw us in fog all the way from Prince Rupert until we reached

Tacoma to load at the Hooker plant, and during the entire trip we seldom saw our barge. While at Tacoma we fuelled up in fog while waiting for the ISLAND PINE to complete loading, and left Tacoma again in fog, which did not clear until we passed Kelsey Bay, on northern Vancouver Island.

Island Tug had several railcar barges, on a number of services around Puget Sound and in the Straits of Georgia, one of which was the ISLAND SPRUCE. She was about 300 ft. long and carried about 2500 tons of liquid caustic soda below deck with railcars on deck. I had command of the LLOYD B. GORE, a big, almost ocean going tug with plenty of power having a 1250 h.p. Superior diesel. This combination was on the run to Port Alice around Cape Scott. We carried loaded chlorine tank cars, and general cargo box cars for loading whale meat, destined for California, at the Coal Harbour whaling station. Every possible precaution had to be taken in making the cars secure for the trip as we were going out into the open Pacific, and into sea conditions about as bad as anyone could confront anywhere in the North Pacific.

Loading required the use of heavy turnbuckles at each corner of the car, jacks placed underneath each car to counteract the turnbuckles, wheel stops and heavy chains attached to the main deck, which were in turn secured to the axles. Each line of cars was attached to a coupler on the high bulkhead formed by the forecastle and finally each car was individually braked with air and hand brakes. One would think that, short of the vessel itself sinking, nothing could happen to these rail cars considering how tightly they were secured, but believe it or not, damage could and did occur from time to time, as I will recount later.

Heading north we reached Goletas Channel which one could call the northernmost part of the east side of Vancouver Island. The next stop, weather and tide permitting, was to cross the treacherous Nahwitti Bar and after that it was open Pacific water, around Cape Scott, until we reached the entrance of Quatsino Sound on our way into Port Alice. We arrived on one occasion in the Goletas to find several other tows all awaiting weather improvement, with a 65-70 mph southeasterly. Island Tug was well represented with an empty paper barge, the regular freight barge in charge of the ISLAND WARRIOR and a couple of log barges all of which circling behind their respective tugs. Vancouver Tug was represented by two barges waiting to make it to Port Alice.

After five days there seemed to be some moderation in the weather as the forecast was for improvement as the wind went round to the north west, so two of the tows including our regular freight barge sneaked out quickly and made Port Alice. The Nahwitti, even by itself, was a challenge and considering the nature of our deck load, including about 14 loaded chlorine tank cars, discretion told me to take the longer route around to the east of Nigei Island, in the equally stormy but deep water Queen Charlotte Sound, which at least enabled us to avoid the broadside buffeting involving in crossing the shallow Nahwitti Bar.

Once we got out off the north coast at the point of no return, the wind changed back to gale force South East. We took a terrible pounding at reduced speed, as in spite of weather reports conditions simply worsened. At times we lost sight of the barge as we fell into deep troughs, and then we would ride up like a roller coaster and catch a glimpse of our barge behind us, ploughing deep into green water which

Serenading the tourists aboard the SEA LION.
The author working the controls of the air whistle, while playing a tuneful melody to passengers aboard an incoming P & O cruise liner.

cascaded over the forecastle and flooded down among the railway cars to rid itself over the side like a miniature Niagara Falls.

At other times the barge would throw her bulk up in the air, exposing a hundred feet of her bottom before she plunged down into the next trough, like a plunging whale. If one was frightened this was the time to be so affected, and I could hardly blame a man who felt fear of nature's conditions.

We reached Port Alice and in spite of every loading precaution with the cars, jacks had crumpled, chains had broken and turnbuckles had been wrenched free. We lost no cars, but that was one of the worst dustings I ever experienced.

I guess any one who knows Quatsino Narrows will know how narrow and tortuous a channel it really is, requiring great care in making its passage. The entrance to the narrows is made passing islands and rocks on the south side, and the old settlement of Quatsino on the north side. Then a ninety degree turn has to be executed usually against a fast ebbtide for easier handling. The Narrows proper are about half the width of the channel we know as the Lions Gate, but suddenly once through into Holberg Inlet the entire landscape changes and it almost feels like a lake. I should say, by the way, that I have never seen so many eagles as can be found perched in trees overlooking the narrows. They sit there, perhaps a hundred or so at a time, awaiting the chance to swoop down and snatch a salmon which is scooped up at tremendous speed. So certain are they of their prowess that the process appears to be almost effortless as a large salmon suddenly finds itself out of its element and zooming 200 feet up in the air.

On one occasion we were heading for Coal Harbour at the south end of Holberg Inlet, in the early hours of the morning. We were watching our radar closely, but sought a light which should have been visible. We could not see it and quickly realised why, as we had entered a solid bank of fog, which I first noticed swirling over our sidelights. As we went into the narrow channel with a now invisible barge riding behind us, it was a bit of an eerie feeling. I was at the open window and periodically sounding the whistle for echoes, a deckhand had the wheel while the mate was watching the radar, now of little use in these very close quarters.

Suddenly the young deckhand said "Jeez. I'm scared".

I said to him, "Don't be scared son, you're doing just fine. The time to be scared is when you see me scared". Such is the nature of giving out moral strength at the right time!

Coal Harbour in those days was the site of an active whaling station, where B.C. Packers and Taiyo Fishing, a Japanese company ran a joint venture operation. It was fascinating to watch the dexterity of the three or four men at work on the carcass as they stripped the animal of its flesh with their long flensing knives, but I certainly did not like what I saw, when I thought of these magnificent animals, which we saw so often from our towboats, being stripped for their fat, oils, and meat, with all the waste being rendered into meal or fertiliser. It was a tragedy that has happily ended at least on the B.C. coast, and I hope it never revives.

Not many people can appreciate the point that Vancouver Island actually has a north coast. We tend to think in terms of the east and the west coasts only, perhaps thinking of Vancouver Island as lying where it does shaped like a gigantic sweet potato with a pointed end at each extremity. Take a look at the map and note that from the Nahwitti Bar to Cape Scott there actually is a north coast, without shelter and more often than not storm wracked. There are a few indentations such as the mouth of the Nahwitti River, one of only two sizeable rivers entering the sea via the north coast, as well as Shuttleworth Bight, Nissen, Nels and Experiment Bights by which time one is up to Cape Scott, an axeshaped headland that pokes into the Pacific. As one rounds Cape Scott there are two offshore islands, the Scott Islands, which form a pass between themselves and the cape. These are the home of seabirds, and as the course is shaped back to a south-southeasterly in the direction of Quatsino Sound you pass Hansen Lagoon and San Josef Bay.

There have been many shipwrecks over the years on the west coast of Vancouver Island and the severe conditions around Cape Scott have claimed many vessels and lives. A few railway cars lie on the bottom there also, and probably the largest wreck I can remember in recent years was that of the almost new log barge RIVTOW NORSEMAN of the Rivtow Straits fleet, in October 1971. Fully laden

Diesel Tug LLOYD B. GORE
Former Young & Gore flagship. A powerful member of the Island Tug Fleet, and a favourite with the author.

with a capacity load of logs, she was evidently swept up on one of the Scott Islands after her tow line broke in treacherous conditions such as we had just experienced. She was pounded to pieces in just a few short hours. The other was the coastal freighter NORTHOLM owned by Northland Transportation which foundered in heavy seas off Cape Scott with the loss of all but two crewmen aboard sometime in the fifties, when we were actually weatherbound in Safety Cove on the other side of Queen Charlotte Sound.

Reputedly there are ghosts at Cape Scott, according to what I have been told by fellow towboat masters. One such, who visits passing vessels, is a mysterious figure wearing a sou'wester and black wetweather gear, who has been seen grasping the deck rails outside the wheelhouse. I have not had the experience personally and pass this all on without theorising or comment. There does not however seem to be anything sinister about such visitations, and good friends who have had the experience have told it to me in all sincerity. Evidently there are "good" and "bad" ghosts connected with the sea, and those of Cape Scott appear to be in the first category, perhaps coming to the aid of mariners exposed to danger.

From the sea the land forms a low only slightly undulating landscape, as there are no high mountains at the north end of the island. I am told that the land itself is muskeg over very large areas, with scrubby low grade timber, but here and there one can find quite good natural pasture. This wet, usually cold lowland was quite unlike most of the rest of Vancouver Island except for such smaller areas as the south side of the mouth of Kyuquot Sound. It is interesting because not only does it have much in common with the Falkland Islands and Patagonia at the southern end of Argentina, but as happened in those countries, at the end of the last century and up until the first world war it attracted settlers of Scandinavian and British origin, who were encouraged to go there by settlement societies.

Settlement of vacant remote lands seemed to be the objective at all costs of our Victorian ancestors, the attraction held out of course, being land so cheap that it was virtually available for free. To say the very least, they must have been a hardy bunch. Typical for example, is the story of the Danes who carried a piano by shear human muscle all the way from San Josef at the head of Holberg Inlet through fallen timber, across creeks and muskegs to their settlement at Hansen Lagoon.

Another story involves an English group who landed through the surf from the Boscowitz steamer at the mouth of the Nahwitti, complete with piano, ladies in long dresses and broad brimmed hats. There was no shelter, so the men turned to with axes and saws to set up a tent camp in time for nightfall while their animals were tethered in a rough corral. When the first world war arrived most of these settlement groups, particularly the Nahwitti settlement, eroded away as the menfolk joined the army, some to die in France, while the women and children returned to Vancouver. The Scandinavian settlements lingered on for some time, but as the next generation came along, the need for self-betterment and education, and a variety of creature comforts ensured that there would be few in the next generation to follow the lead of the first generation.

There must have been something good about the life, as apparently long after the last settlers had left, wild descendents of the original cattle could still be found surviving in the bush. By now most of the settlement lands have reverted to the crown, and much of it has been incorporated into the Cape Scott Provincial Park.

On one occasion we were towing a railbarge up to Ucluelet and had a young new deckhand on board who came from the prairies. When we were coming up to Sheringham Point he was quite intrigued with some porpoise. Then we saw a large basking shark and I pointed this out to him without realising just what effect that this would have on him.

I said, "this would not be a good time to fall overboard" with which, I guess he agreed. When we got back to Vancouver he announced that he was quitting, so I asked him "why?".

He replied, "if I have to sail around with things like that for company" referring to the shark, "I'm going back to the prairies" which so far as I know is what he did.

I remember another incident which had a touch of the ludicrous to it. On this occasion we were near Stillwater on our way to Prince Rupert with a chemical barge for Columbia Cellulose. The mate drew my attention to a small boat apparently with no one on board, drifting some little way off. We changed course to investigate, and as we closed with the boat we noticed a body lying sprawled inside the boat. We managed to bring it alongside so that the mate could hop down and check out the body. As it turned out the body was very much alive and looking like a boiled lobster in the hot sun. When he woke up, he was angry at having been disturbed in his very drunken snooze. In fact, he was pretty rude at our intrusion, but with a 300 foot barge hanging off our stern we did not want to hang around in any event. We got under way, but radioed the R.C.M.P. at Powell River.

They responded, and in about another half hour they called us from their vessel to say that they had found the boat and had "got their man". As I noted earlier, booze and boats do not make a good safe mix!

By the way, on this trip we had taken the less usual course of heading through Yuculta Rapids, which is quite passable in the right conditions for large vessels such as our barge. It has the advantage of avoiding the heavy tide of lower Johnstone Straits and the Seymour Narrows, and is a little shorter. However, these big shipshaped barges were towed off a single chain rigged to the stem, and had a nasty habit of yawing badly at times when towed against a tide. It was made worse if they had not been trimmed exactly right. With a rectangular shaped barge with a rake going across the entire width of the vessel, it was a lot easier to handle the tow, as the towing bridle was rigged to both outer extremities of the barge.

By now it was 1969 and I was 51 years old. It came as a complete surprise, while on a 24 hour home leave when I had planned to go into the city with Eunice to look after a few personal matters, to receive a call from Don Elworthy in the Vancouver office of Island Tug to go in as he wished to see me. Don was the middle son of Harold Elworthy and was very well thought of as a towboat executive both inside and outside the company. What he had on his mind was to ask me if I would be interested in coming ashore and taking an office job.

This was something I had never ever considered, but at my age, I had to admit to myself that I was starting to feel a few of the aches and pains of past injuries, and climbing up on the roof of ice covered boxcars and jumping from one to the other was starting to pall a little. I told Don that I could not give him an immediate answer, as I needed a little time to think it over, and in any event I wanted to discuss it with my wife before reaching a decision. I told him I was due to go out again on the LLOYD B. GORE at midnight, but he was a step ahead of me.

"Don't you worry about that" he said, "another master is taking her out tonight so you take two weeks off with pay and let me have your answer when you can".

This offer had opened up all sorts of cross currents. I had been at sea since leaving school, and ships and saltchuck were in my blood. I went home and told Eunice who listened patiently, as usual to everything I had to say but offered no opinion. We went to bed that night with the matter still very heavily on my conscience, but by morning my mind was made up. I told her that I had made my decision and was going to take the offer.

It was only then that Eunice revealed her feelings in the matter, as she wept tears of joy. She was so pleased with my choice after all these years of having me away more often than I was at home.

"I was not going to pass any opinion which might influence you" she said, "as I know how important the life at sea has been for you. If I had said anything I might have been accused of putting pressure on you, and I did not want that to happen".

The job provided the equivalent of my master's pay with some added bonuses such as car and entertainment allowance. Moreover, I was able to get home every night with the exception of the odd short business trip to Vancouver Island or down to the U.S. I was one of four former towboat masters working out of the office, and we all had accounts to look after. My responsibility was the log and bulk cargo divisions, and as such, I looked after and was in close touch with such major accounts as McMillan, Bloedel, Domtar Ltd. and B.C. Forest Products, for whom we towed out of Nitinat Lake and Port Renfrew. The job included being a trouble shooter and making sure that our services were handled efficiently, and at all times to their satisfaction.

We had two offices, the one in Victoria being head office, while our Vancouver based towboat operations were serviced from the former Pacific Drydock location in North Vancouver. The main Vancouver office was for many years located in the Marine Building and later in the Bentall Centre.

I was becoming quite used to the job and enjoying it very much, getting to know and entertaining all those customers for whom I was responsible, along with a great many people in the office who had previously been names at best. I found them to be a grand crowd, and I still have many happy memories of that period.

The news of a merger with Vancouver Tugboat Company came very suddenly and rather disturbingly for some of us. We wondered what kind of an animal the new Vanisle Tug & Barge would be, as here were the two largest towboat companies in B.C. getting together and forming a giant. This will be the subject of the next chapter, but before moving on I just want to record the fact that in Island Tug & Barge, a man could not have a finer employer. They were fair and reasonable at all times, they backed me to the hilt, and most importantly, listened to the advice of their masters, always leaving something in reserve and avoiding driving their people to the breaking point as had happened elsewhere.

The waterfront was as surprised as we were, and I do not doubt that there was much speculation on what kind of "marriage", this would turn out to be, and who would wear the pants in the new operation!

Chapter Eleven

The Big Merger

Mergers in business are a lot like marriages. Some are successful, and some should just never have happened. Some people gain very substantially, and some are hurt but almost inevitably there are, in every case, growing pains which have to be allowed for.

The motivations for mergers do vary over a wide spectrum. The first objective is usually to strengthen the new corporate vessel so that the total will become greater than the sum of its individual parts, and while for legal purposes one company may technically buy out the other or alternatively the assets of both partners are put together, so far as the original shareholders in the merging partners are concerned, in a commonly-owned new corporate vehicle, a merger remains a marriage of relative equals and is not a buyout or takeover of a lesser or weaker company, which might have fallen by the wayside, again for many good and valid reasons.

Ever since the authors have been in business, and most particularly in the postwar period, mergers in business in Canada have made commercial news on a consistant basis, not just in the transportation industry but in most others as well. Back in the fifties the Bank of Toronto and the Dominion Bank of Canada successfully merged to form today's powerful and successful Toronto-Dominion Bank, and as it is understood, this was a marriage of relative equals who did what made logical business sense and created a vehicle of greater strength, better able to compete with the other big Canadian banks.

MacMillan & Bloedel merged with the Powell River Company in the sixties again in a marriage which made a lot of strategic sense within the forest industry, but created considerable unease in the newly merged company. MacMillan, which about two decades earlier merged more happily with Bloedel Stewart & Welch, being the more powerful and aggressive partner, left its stamp on everything in no uncertain way with most of the top jobs going to MacMillan executives. The few which went to Powell River people did not last as they quickly vacated them in the face of internal personality pressures. Both companies tended to be controlled by strong men at the top, but whereas MacMillan had always adopted an aggressive expansive posture, the Powell River people, while more than capable, seemed to have gone into the merger for more defensive reasons.

The towboat industry has seen many buyouts up to recent times, and most frequently these have usually been a straight purchase of assets and goodwill by a strong buyer from a weaker seller. Straits Towing seemed to start the post war towboat industry's expansion binge when the dominant McKeen interests in that company, purchased control of Union Steamships in 1955. Soon after it acquired control of Pacific Coyle Navigation in 1956. This was a towboat company owning for the most part out of date vessels, whose management also had not grown with the times in aggressively updating its physical plant and seeking new business.

Island Tug & Barge somewhat later acquired Young & Gore Ltd. (1952) and Victoria Tugboats (1959) as had Vancouver Tugboat Company purchased Dolmage Towing and Western Tug & Barge, both in 1956, Vancouver Barge Transportation in 1962 and Pacific Tanker Company in 1964. So far as is known most were simply ready to honourably retire from the business. Vancouver Barge's days were numbered on account of curtailment of its services caused by the spreading growth of the B.C. Ferry System, who provided better ferry services on all major routes, and many minor ones as well.

These all seem to be natural consequences in small private companies where ownership is concentrated with one man or a very small family group. Heirs and successors do not always have the drive or foresight to take over where the founder left off and conservative thinking sometimes prevents the company growing with the times. No provision is made for succession in both management and ownership and a level of development and even competence, is not reached where a really well-motivated and efficient management structure remains, once the original driving force passes on.

Another factor of critical importance has been the ever present temptation to over-expand beyond a smaller company's capital resources. A good example of this was M.R. Cliff Towing, an old established log tower of some size, which went on an expansion binge in the fifties, spending a lot of money on fancy new corporate headquarters, buying an elderly Great Lakes vessel for conversion to a log barge, among re-enginings and the like, as they sought to break out of straight flat boom towing upon which their business had been built. The former lakes steamer was lost soon after conversion to the log barge, LOG TRANSPORTER. The company went bankrupt with its assets passing to others within the industry.

Purists frequently contend that mergers within an industry lessen competition, and in some instances this is very true. In the case of the B.C. towboat and coastal transportation industry, many factors were at play during the fifties and sixties. Comprehensive Union Steamship Company services were to become a thing of the past by about the end of the fifties, as in fact was to become the case with Canadian National Railways steamship service on the Prince Rupert run. Canadian Pacific Steamship services between the mainland and Vancouver Island were not moving with the times. With improving road systems the ferry services came to be viewed as an integral part of the highway system. Beautiful and dignified old coastal liners were not the way to go, supported as they were by generally outmoded facilities.

Services to more far flung coastal points were provided by Northland Navigation Company with the aid of government subsidies, but as these latter tended to erode away, the Northland company, in its final years controlled by Phs. Van Ommeren of Holland, followed its predecessors in the coastal liner business to eventual extinction. There seems to be little doubt that the B.C. government's growing monopoly of passenger and roll-on roll-off ferry services was an important factor in the demise of all of the predecessor services. There was, however, another fallout which developed from the growth of the ferry system, and that was that population centres which could be reached by road and/or ferry prospered greatly. The ripple effect of economic activity created beneficial effects for the towboat industry which developed new lines of freight handling activity as the coast forestry and mining industries grew.

By the late sixties the big five companies, Island Tug & Barge, Vancouver Tug Boat Company, Straits Towing, Rivtow Marine and Gulf of Georgia Towing Company had probably reached their optimum size as individual units and quite likely also, some of the competition they were generating was proving to be wasteful. Straits and Rivtow merged together in the first of a succession of major moves which would leave two large surviving companies, but more about this topic later.

The merger between Island Tug & Barge and Vancouver Tugboat Company was the second and larger of the two major industry mergers and precisely what esoteric reasons motivated it, have not been revealed to the public at large. Increasing concentration in the forest industry might have had a peripheral influence, in that big business tends to work more with big service business and appreciates that the mammoth capital investment required to service the needs of big business must either come from its own sources or be provided through a strong and well capitalised service industry. Big business tends toward monopoly and equally finds that beyond a certain point its interests are better served by having perhaps two large well founded and efficient service businesses to serve its needs, leaving a competition factor in place rather than five or more smaller firms all yapping at its heels as they scramble for business.

Island Tug and VanTug were certainly in neither instance likely to take a back seat to anyone else in terms of being well established, and strongly managed, but both had for years been dominated by strong men who ran their operations in ways that differed and gave each company a distinct personality. Harold Elworthy had started Island Tug in 1925 from very small beginnings in Victoria, and the modern VanTug business went back to 1924, when it was restarted by the original founder's son and daughter, Harold and Ruth, and from then on never looked back. After the death of Harold Jones in 1956, management passed to Arthur Lindsay his partner, J.C.F. "Jim" Stewart, and Arthur's son Rod Lindsay.

Harold Elworthy had three sons all of whom held major executive positions in Island Tug. Although founded by Elworthy the company did pass into the control of A.C. Burdick of Pacific Drydock and Pacific Salvage and for a period Elworthy had partnered Senator S.S. McKeen in developing Straits Towing. Differences between these two strong men resulted in Elworthy returning to Island Tug & Barge, which became an Elworthy family concern for many years although later Foss Tug and Launch Company of Seattle acquired an interest. For several years prior to the founding of Seaspan it had been controlled by McAllister Bros. Towing of New York and Montreal, a company which in turn was controlled by a Belgian investment group operating in Canada as Sogemines. Behind Sogemines was an array of some of the most powerful Belgian banking and industrial companies, such as that country's largest banking concern, Societe General and Union Miniere de Haut Katanga, a giant mining group. In fact consideration of the name "Sogemines" reveals that it is contrived from the names of the above two concerns.

VanTug was strongly controlled by Harold Jones to the time of his death in December 1956, but in July of that year as noted earlier, it had acquired Dolmage Towing, another well managed company headed, and dominated by Captain Bill Dolmage. Dolmage Towing had a strong position in log towing and the new acquisition was renamed Vancouver Log Towing Company. This purchase had taken place during one of the most intense expansionist periods in the coastal economy, with a new aluminum smelter, and new pulp and paper mills under construction at several places quite apart from the rebuilding of older facilities. This growth was at the core of much additional expansion in almost every other conceivable direction on the coast. No doubt the acquisition of the Dolmage fleet was a quick and relatively cheap way of acquiring a lot of ready built towing power almost overnight, compared to a long-term and costly new building program.

Chip barges already in short supply, could not be purchased out of any second hand pool, so VanTug was also faced with quickly building and financing a series of ten new chip barges to fill an increasing shortage of equipment in servicing their contracts.

It was really a matter that as fast as the company made a dollar, it had to commit to three more, but the untimely death of Mr. Jones created additional complications. Matters were assisted when a group of Vancouver businessmen arranged to make an investment which enabled the company to meet expansion plans.

The day was saved. Vantug had added the Dolmage fleet, was now assured of meeting its contractual chip barge committments to its major forestry clients, and the financial fabric of the company had been improved simultaneously. However this was really only a temporary answer because the demands of industries which the towboat companies sought to meet did not in any way diminish.

Towboat managements wrestled with the multiple problems of an essentially capital intensive, low net-return industry, fairly typical of the transportation sector generally. New union agreements, new manning requirements, higher horsepower and better constructional standards all conspired to add to the capital cost of new tugs in particular, and higher deadweight and more sophisticated cargo handling requirements did the same for barges.

Both authors well remember the challenges and constraints placed on towboat managers when they were in the towboat business themselves and with the far larger companies under discussion here, problems multiplied as their needs were vastly greater, and yet essentially they still only had access to private capital sources and bank funding, both of which have limitations. When under private ownership Vantug and Island Tug faced similar problems, without in any way implying any management or motivational shortcomings. In fact their problems were the same as those of the rest of the industry which was how to finance expansion and stay in control of the ship, and much credit must go to the industry at large for the very high Canadian investment content and relatively small foreign involvement which has been a feature of coastal transportation.

During the sixties control of Island Tug had passed to McAllister Brothers which, as already noted, was controlled by Sogemines, a Belgian controlled company, and rather later control in VanTug passed to the Dillingham Corporation of Hawaii. These similar moves both took their managements into a broader international arena and the stage was clearly set for a new phase of industry rationalisation and consolidation.

As noted the first newsworthy event was the merger between Straits Towing Ltd., a public company controlled by the McKeen interests and their allies, and Rivtow, a fast rising privately owned conglomeration of towboat companies dominated by the Cosulich Brothers. Within weeks the announcement was made of the merger of Island Tug and VanTug which came out under the cumbersome name of VanIsle Tug & Barge. Aside from the fact that this was an even bigger merger than that of Rivtow Straits Ltd. the new name seemed to have a negative impact on the business world and some short time later the new, and far more impressive name "Seaspan International" came onto the local and international towing scene.

The new merger was impressive to say the least. The two largest towboat companies in Canada had now become an even larger international organisation. In the process of emerging the Dillingham interests bowed out and it become a wholly owned subsidiary of Sogemines, soon to be renamed Genstar Corporation. The total number of tugs at the time of the merger was 65 with a further 250 barges of various types. As time progressed the fleet was greatly rationalised with much older and obsolescent equipment being weeded out and replaced by new higher horsepower tugs and larger capacity barges so at the present time the fleet numbers 45 tugs and 225 barges. It dominated some sectors of the towboat business if not completely, then almost so, and controlled a large part of the remainder with the exception of log flat boom towing which had been a diminishing interest of both companies for some years.

One of the assets brought to the merger by VanTug was Vancouver Shipyards Ltd. a far sighted acquisition made by the company in the Harold Jones era, when the need for a new home was foreseen for the company's repair yard in Coal Harbour. The mounting pressures of Vancouver real estate development could be guaranteed to eventually consume its Coal Harbour ship repair location. With extensive and modern shipbuilding and repair facilities, the present site of Vancouver Shipyards, which it shares with Seaspan, gives a secure home base for both companies for many years to come.

From what can be determined, the dovetailing of the two organisations was handled with the minimum of dislocation and hurt feelings. Inevitably the company did not need two of everything when clearly one was called for, and this applied equally to humans as it did to physical assets. Natural attrition and retirements took care of many situations, and there is no recollection of employees simply leaving the company out of dissatisfaction with the merger even though patience had to undoubtedly be exercised by some. Island Tug's Point Ellis shipyard, its West Bay Rail Terminal, and the Island Tug head office at Victoria were all phased out, but the Elworthys reacquired the popular PRINCESS MARY restaurant as a private investment. This had been a significant profit centre in the old days of Island Tug, but would clearly not now fit the new concept of Seaspan International.

At the top though, VanTug appeared to come off a little better than Island Tug, with Jim Stewart as the new president and Arthur Elworthy as chairman of the board. A management shuffle saw Mr. Elworthy retire by 1973 with Mr. Stewart moving to chairman of the board and Rod Lindsay taking over as president. Unfortunately, Mr. Lindsay was not able to enjoy his new position for very long as he suffered a fatal heart attack right at his prime. He was not the first to succumb prematurely in an industry which, with its stresses and strains, tended to be a man-killer. However, when Ross Turner was brought into the company to head Seaspan,

Motor Tug ATTA BOY
The first unit in the fleet of Vancouver Tugboat Company. VanTug was re-established by Harold Jones in 1924, thus pre-dating Island Tug & Barge by one year. ATTA BOY was therefore also the first of the vast fleets which followed and eventually became Seaspan International Ltd.

his annealing abilities appeared to settle many matters in the executive suite and the company went from strength to strength.

There were two further significant mergers after Seaspan came into being. One was the takeover of F.M. Yorke & Sons Ltd. who had a strong position in railcar barging to Vancouver Island, possessing a small fleet of excellent modern vessels. The second merger settled the issue of what the future held for the fifth of the big five companies, existing to the Straits Rivtow merger.

This company, Gulf of Georgia Towing Co. Ltd., had expanded like the others at a headlong pace since the close of the second world war, and was now seen as something of a "loose cannon" within the industry. It had originally specialised in river and harbour movements of sawn lumber to and from mills, and alongside export ships with a large fleet of wooden scows, but like others it had anticipated many changes and had steadily re-equipped itself with a substantial fleet of steel barges, new tugs, and had broken into long distance towing and the movement of petroleum and other bulk products. Headed by James S. Byrn, the third generation in the ownership and management of the company, it was well regarded as being an efficient operation but like others, management had found that financing newer and larger equipment to meet the demands of industry was becoming very wearing, quite apart from the danger of being shut off from further growth by its two huge competitors. Mr. Byrn responded to an attractive offer and became president of Genstar Marine until his retirement. Genstar Marine was then the parent of Seaspan International, and Vancouver Shipyards ran as a separate entity, but the two taken together constituted the marine division of the parent Genstar Corporation.

For a period Genstar Marine operated an international division with a few powerful tugs and ten oversize barges engaged around the world wherever suitable contracts could be found, but in practice this proved to be a difficult market in which to function and with the breakup of the parent Genstar, these vessels were sold off and the division discontinued.

Seaspan also entered into a number of joint ventures with partners like Federal Commerce & Navigation Company of Montreal, a Canadian deepsea shipowning concern, and Crowley Maritime Inc. of San Francisco a large American company with big interests in both towing and deepsea operations, and Union Remarque de Sauvetage, a Belgian salvage concern. These alliances in one way and another, extended the Seaspan involvements into the Arctic, North Sea and Middle East. With the exception of the Arctic, the company is now out of its foreign joint ventures.

Shortly after Seaspan was named another corporate change took place in that its parent changed its name from Sogemines to Genstar Corporation, to which by now, Ross Turner had been elevated along with Angus McNaughton, and so commenced the rapid expansion of Genstar as a major conglomerate enterprise with widespread interests across Canada and the U.S., but during the eighties the end for Genstar was looming.

Genstar had been building an important financial services division and had secured control of the large Canada Permanent Mortgage and Trust Corporations. Probably the matter of Genstar's future might have rested there undisturbed, but a critical move was made when Genstar went after Canada Trust, the country's largest trust company, in competition with Imasco Ltd. an even larger conglomerate which had been built out of the old Imperial Tobacco Company.

From an onlooker's point of view, the struggle between Genstar and Imasco was rather like a battle of the titans. Genstar had bested Imasco in the fight for Canada Trust, but Imasco in a move taking financial markets by surprise, secured control of Genstar keeping those components it needed and selling off the rest, including its Seaspan and Vancouver Shipyards investments. A local group of Vancouver businessmen including MacLuan Capital group purchased the company from Genstar in 1987 and thus control returned to Vancouver based interests.

British Columbia's towboat industry had always been highly fluid. In spite of the seeming hegemony of the two super companies, Seaspan International and Rivtow Straits, smaller concerns have managed to not only survive but also prosper. Readers will recall that the first Pacific Towing Company was an associate of Dola Towing as mentioned earlier in this book, but one such prosperous survivor is the second "Pacific Towing", Pacific Towing Services Ltd. headed by Ron Wilson, and there are others such as Hodder, Noble, Valley, Harken, Stradiotti and North Arm Transportation to name but a few.

What can the future hold for all of them large and small? Who is to tell? The major forest companies, MacMillan Bloedel, Fletcher Challenge and Weldwood all have marine divisions or subsidiaries, but there are many uncertainties and when changes do come they are often very surprising as indeed was the "big merger" of Island Tug & Barge and Vancouver Tugboat Companyback in 1971.

Chapter Twelve

My Years with Seaspan International Ltd.

Having been employed by both Island Tug & Barge and Vancouver Tugboat Company it was inevitable that comparisons would be made as the new Seaspan organisation took form.

Island Tug's corporate personality was highly respected I believe, with a strong feeling of both stability and integrity. Harold Elworthy was highly regarded in and out of the business and under his guidance the company had grown steadily with no internal corporate eruptions which the outside world ever heard of, if indeed they ever occurred. Moreover, he had developed a team of executives who were not exceeded in capability elsewhere, and the corporate thrust reflected itself in the handling of its seagoing staff, where the attitude always was that if a master had something to say, he was listened to. In short I believe teamwork was always the watchword in Island Tug and it reflected itself at every level of the organisation.

Vancouver Tugboat Company has always operated as a very aggressive and successful organisation and like Island Tug had more than any other company built itself a powerful position as a mover of bulk materials such as wood chips, bulk chemicals and petroleum products together with mill products such as pulp and paper. It was probably dominant in the movement of wood chips, but had not established a strong position for itself in railcar barging and was only scratching the surface of log barging. The company was known to take shortcuts to achieve an objective and this placed a lot of stress on seagoing staff where the master was not always encouraged to exercise his own better judgement.

At first we functioned as VanIsle Tug & Barge, which was believed by most to be simply an interim name. When the new name "Seaspan International" was announced, there came a renaming of every vessel in the fleet. All barges now carried a new Seaspan name as fast as they could be painted on their hulls. I.T.& B No. 100 or VT 88 became SEASPAN 100 or SEASPAN 88. The former Island Tug towboats were easily renamed by substituting the prefix "Seaspan" for "Island", so that ISLAND SOVEREIGN became SEASPAN SOVEREIGN, but the French styling of Vancouver Tugboat with its "La" and "Le" as in LA REINE involved more rearrangement with names in most instances where appropriate being translated into their English equivalent. A new corporate emblem and new tug and barge liveries were adopted to a distinct styling which could not be confused with that of any other transportation company. This transition was handled with great expertise and the employees had a new sense of purpose which helped get rid of the personality quirks of "ex-Island Tug" and "ex-VanTug". Moreover our customers and the public at large had a new easily recognised organisation to conjure with and I believe that it was received readily and with satisfaction by all concerned.

During Island Tug days we had purchased our retirement home at Boundary Bay and with the hours I put in as an account executive it worked out quite well, but with the merger now announced many things were to change. Once the merger was set up a great many jobs also changed so a big meeting was called of all affected personnel, and out of the new appointments I was to be "Safety and Training Officer", a new function which I did not find hard to take as I had always followed an interest in running a well found ship, and of course we now had a huge fleet of tugs to look after, not to mention a personnel list which had doubled in size. The only problem I had was that my salary was considerably lower than in Island Tug, but one had to be patient as there were a half million things to be ironed out in establishing a new organisation like Seaspan.

The first thing to do was to get busy and get to know the various masters and crews. I started off with meetings with the masters, then the mates, followed by engineers and then the seamen. These meetings were informal and informative as I got to know of their problems, complaints and suggestions as to how they felt about a whole host of matters of concern to them. It also provided the opportunity to let them know how I proposed to pursue my new responsibilities and encourage safer working practices.

Of necessity these meetings had to go on for some weeks, as it was impossible to bring everyone in at the same time as there were always about half of our personnel out on actual duty aboard the boats. Nevertheless this task was accomplished and much of value came out of them.

Out of this came a seaman's course lasting one week when we went over the whole process of safe working practices on the job, wire and rope splicing, bends and hitches, a St. John's Ambulance course and regulatory subjects concerning company policies and other subjects. I brought a senior master ashore for the purpose and it worked out very well both as a refresher course for experienced personnel and as an introduction for the many new deckhands we were hiring and training.

Masters and their mates being human, do not always get along too well, personality problems being typical. When this happened, I was sometimes confronted with the need to have our personnel department arrange a judicious switch of the mate to another vessel. After all, if a master and mate cannot work together, teamwork is going to suffer and as the reader will remember from my account of docking railcar barges, co-operation and complete understanding as between master and mate are essential to a well operated tug and tow.

Some of the senior masters were not too happy about these meetings which they were required to attend. In spite of long experience, a man who does not keep abreast of developments quickly finds that his experience is not sufficient to enable him to stay up to date particularly in a vigorous new organisation.

I had people from our marine insurance brokers come to meetings and explain the intricacies of marine insurance and how it served the overall Seaspan operation. I made similar arrangements with our corporate law firm who sent their maritime law specialists who explained the legal intricacies, how they affected the masters and how to minimise the company's exposure to litigation. Other outside people came including the Workmen's Compensation Board who approved of everything which was being done to promote safe working conditions. On other occasions, we had the Canadian Coastguard along and their American equivalent from the Thirteenth United States Coast Guard (USCG) District in Seattle. Overall this program worked very well because it gave the masters an opportunity to see and appreciate many factors in the operations of the company which normally were seldom

SEASPAN SOVEREIGN
Salvaged by Island Tug & Barge as a wreck in Johnstone Straits. Rebuilt as ISLAND SOVEREIGN and still an efficient member of today's Seaspan fleet over forty years later.

revealed in this manner to seagoing personnel. Personally, I think it added to the sum total of teamwork and was an improver of morale.

A problem which did develop and put a strain on our operating personnel afloat was the habit of some departments to put pressure on the master to highball an assignment. This was showing up adversely in more minor accidents, in berthing, and in barge handling which might result in damage to the barge. In most cases nothing very serious happened, but it remains costly in terms of repair work and downtime out of service and, of course, we always had to be mindful of our insurance record. Underwriters were there to cover serious loss and certainly did not want to finance maintainance with petty claims. Quite apart from that, the annual cost of paying the premium on our hull and machinery coverage for the entire fleet came to an enormous sum. This was not my department, but it takes almost nothing to understand that if a fleet rate is say 2 percent annually, an increase to 2.5 percent represents a 20 percent increase. The premium on a million dollar vessel could then jump from $20,000 to $25,000, so multiply that by a fleet numbering in the several hundreds of vessels and it all represents very big money.

A lot of our tows were into Puget Sound ports and for a while the company was getting frequent notifications from the USCG Puget Sound vessel traffic system with complaints about infractions of pilotage rules, most commonly lack of attention to strict requirements on the separation of inward and outward vessel traffic. I made frequent visits to the headquarters of the USCG Thirteenth District in Seattle in an effort to improve relationships between them, the company and our own masters.

Complaints of this type gave the company a bad name with an important organisation who could not be ignored. A complaint would reach the company and come to my desk for action. Direct discussion did not seem to produce the desired results, nor did open discussion in the masters' meetings, so I arranged through the personnel office that future warnings would go directly from the Coast Guard people to the offending master's home. Needless to say such letters were couched in stern language, having their own special way of implying a threat, so when it arrived in the master's mail box it came as a bit more of a jolt when reading his mail over breakfast. No fines or penalties had yet been levied, but the result was that we saw a considerable reduction in the frequency and scale of these infractions. Some of the masters who were affected quietly went down to Seattle in their own time to straighten out a given matter with the Coast Guard, and this was precisely the positive sort of result I hoped for.

These moves created a lot of goodwill from the USCG towards Seaspan, from the admiral in charge of the 13th District down. Whenever a new regulation was being considered, they did us the great courtesy of letting us know beforehand and seeking our input, inviting us to Seattle for consultations. Before long, the Canadian Coast Guard became very interested as I kept in close contact with them. Later at times, Peter Woodward of the Council of Marine Carriers would accompany me down for these meetings which were very productive.

There was a considerable contrast between the nature and mode of operation in the two coastguard organisations. The USCG basically followed navy lines with admirals down through all ranks more or less common to the U.S. Navy. In fact in time of war its operations were integrated very much into those of the navy alongside which it functioned. It had a sizeable navy of its own with armed patrol and icebreaker vessels and as such it carried a lot of clout. The Canadian Coastguard is more in the nature of a civilian organisation and is of far more recent origin. As such it lacks the military personality of its U.S. counterpart, more in keeping with the Canadian style of doing things. However its duties are basically similar and have been expanded since its inception to include coastal patrolling and vessel traffic control.

It did not have as many departments as the USCG, but one very good move they made was to set up an accident investigation division, which put more teeth into this important policing function. If an accident occurred it became usual to hold an enquiry involving the offending master or company and as a result its recommendations were then forwarded to Ottawa for whatever action they deemed appropriate. This might result in a master or mate having his ticket endorsed or suspended, or a fine against the company involved. As with the American practice, it had the effect of tightening up a lot of sloppy habits on the coast which resulted from a past ineffective supervison.

A good routine which developed with the USCG and the Canadian Coastguard was a joint enquiry on vessel accidents. The company would be present throughout the entire enquiry which inevitably involved the master and usually the mate as well. We were not there to act as advocates for our men. Our role was in a watching capacity which would also serve our own corporate needs in dealing with any offence. We were not there as "spies" in any way and would freely and fully participate in the enquiry, and encourage our men to tell the truth. The size of ships of all types, and the sheer volume of shipping inevitably lead to more complex navigation rules, and the company was able to learn much in these enquiries which it was able to pass on to other masters.

At one time the radar equipment with which the coast guard vessel traffic services worked at Vancouver was of limited range and could only take effect about as far as Cape Roger Curtis on Bowen Island. Commander Jack Cottingham late of the Royal Canadian Navy was a radar expert who was appointed as manager of the Canadian Traffic services. Under him new sophisticated equipment was installed and the traffic control office was set up in the Capilano 100 building at Park Royal, West Vancouver. With this improved surveillance equipment it can now cover the entire gulf area from Victoria to Campbell River and with a similar installation at Prince Rupert a wide area of the coast can be monitored. Those areas not covered by radar were still monitored with a comprehensive radio reporting system. One improvement which it did institute was the adoption of traffic separation lanes from Lions Gate and across English bay and the Gulf. This followed a near disastrous collision between two foreign merchant ships near Spanish Banks some years ago and is a great improvement on previous rules, or I should say lack of them, as in reality pilots of deepsea ships, masters of tugs and all other vessels used to more or less choose the course they wanted, having regard only to the normal considerations of seamanship and the rules of the road.

Needless to say these new technical controls did not please everyone. Some Canadian crews resented these controls on the grounds that "big brother" was watching, and many were the references to George Orwell's classic "1984". The imposition of Canadian rules were voluntary, but in the view of Seaspan were long overdue, so we started having meetings for the Canadian Coast Guard to present their case and gradually the resentment simmered down. However, whether we like it or not technology is here to stay and today's miracle is as out of date as yesterday's newspaper almost before one can think about it. People including myself complain about new-fangled developments, but when you examine our society objectively, technology is our best and really only assurance that we will be able to maintain an acceptable standard of living for our increasing population.

While I enjoyed the job and know a great deal was achieved in this first year, my role was purely advisory. I could recommend to senior management, but had no real authority and was overruled at times in a manner which was highly negative to the results which were in our grasp. It was like being a policeman without the power to arrest or a judge without the power to pass sentence. In certain departments there was sometimes a desire to avoid rocking anyone's boat. A typical situation might be that of a senior master who cloaked himself in a manner of speaking, "in the robes of an old man of the sea". He was past the stage of taking orders or even suggestions from anyone, and he certainly was not going to take suggestions from me, and because he was so senior and had a wonderfully productive career at sea, he was sometimes treated with all the deference of a sort of holy icon. Every large and successful company has people like this. One might almost say, legends in their own time, but in a vaster new organisation like Seaspan where so

SEASPAN KING towing SEASPAN FORESTER in Howe Sound.
The FORESTER is the world's largest towed log barge with a deadweight capacity of 20,000 tons.

many differing personalities had to be welded together as a team as the company shaped itself for the future these types of situations could readily become a serious obstacle.

In other words my job had to have teeth to gain the best effect and frankly I became so discouraged at one point, that I was even considering asking for a reposting to sea. Being a very direct person, I approached senior management and told them how I felt. The matter adjusted itself in due course when I was appointed Port Captain for Seaspan with duties that encompassed what I had already being doing, plus an increased range of responsibilities in other directions. Ever since I had taken the job I had made it my routine to visit each and every one of the tugs on a regular basis to get to know masters and crew personally, which without question paid off. Now I was in a position to require that something which I saw, that I knew to be wrong would now be rectified without question, whereas before I could only make suggestions or recommendations which oftentimes were ignored. Now the chance to rectify many things which I knew needed attention could be accomplished.

One role which I handled was in effect to act as the owner's representative in situations involving accidents in which Seaspan vessels became involved. It was part of my responsibility to thoroughly investigate all accidents of this type and follow through all Coast Guard enquiries, pre-court business and finally the case in court.

"A common site on the Coast"
Three loaded Seaspan chip barges in triple tow behind SEASPAN WARRIOR.

Two which I recall when I was port captain are particularly interesting and will stand recollection. They both involved two of our biggest tugs and barges and hint at the extent to which Seaspan was involved in international trade.

In the first instance the SUDBURY ll with the barge SEASPAN 250 in tow was on course from Beale Quarries on Texada Island, with 10,000 tons of crushed limerock on board, bound for the Columbia River.

The tug and tow had rounded the traffic separation buoy at the entrance to the Straits of Juan de Fuca. First mate Geoff Partington was on watch and had laid a course from Cape Flattery, to proceed south down the Washington west coast.

It was early a.m. on a cloudy but clear morning. The mate noted two vessels on his radar which wcrc approaching the traffic bouy, one (A) inbound from the northwest astern of him and the other (B) approaching from seaward to the west which was well off to his starboard. Midway to Umatilla Light he observed another vessel (C) rounding Cape Flattery astern of him which on his course would become an overtaking vessel. He also noted that by now the inbound vessel (B) from the west would be well astern of his tow.

A short time later the mate became concerned with the fast overtaking vessel (C), which on its present course would pass close between the SUDBURY ll and the shore. A second outbound vessel (D) now became visible on the radar as it cleared Cape Flattery and settled down on a westerly course and again confirmed that (B) would pass well clear of the SUDBURY ll and her tow.

With no vessels ahead the mate at this point went into the chart room and while there felt a severe jar followed by what seemed to be an increase in the engine revolutions. He observed by radar that his barge echo had merged with another at the same time realising that SUDBURY 11 was running free. He sent the deck hand aft to man the winch, stopped the tug's engine, went aft and saw the towline hanging straight over the stern indicating that the towline was now broken. The towline when winched in was severed about 800 feet from the barge coupler, the overall length of tow line paid out at the time being 2400 feet.

In returning to the wheelhouse he heard a "mayday" call from a vessel called the JAPAN POPLAR (vessel B) stating she was in collison with another vessel, was taking on water and required immediate assistance. Arriving back at her tow, the SUDBURY 11, whose master by now had been called, found the Japanese owned bulk-carrier JAPAN POPLAR stopped with the SEASPAN 250's ship shaped bow and foc'sle embedded in her port side just forward of the ship's bridge and some 600 feet aft from the POPLAR's bows. The Japanese ship was taking water and listing to port. A Canadian coastguard cutter which was actually vessel (A) on the radar screen described above, arrived and was joined by a U.S. cutter which had put out from Neah Bay and all concerned assessed the situation. The SEASPAN 250's collision bulkhead was holding and while the barge's bow had cut deeply into the POPLAR, the latter's cross-bulkheads had not been penetrated and were holding so

SEASPAN DORIS
One of two self-propelled railcar barges, acquired by Seaspan following the purchase of F.M. Yorke & Sons Ltd. in 1972.

it was decided to separate the vessels. Upon separation and further inspection the JAPAN POPLAR and the SEASPAN 250 both proceeded under escort for Victoria.

It soon became apparent that respective claims for the heavy damage suffered by both vessels, and the apportionment of blame would have to be settled in court. Pre-trial proceedings started almost immediately and after several months Admiralty court dates were set and hearings commenced with the final decision being 100 per cent in favour of Seaspan.

Evidence given by other vessels in the immediate area was that all navigation lights on both the tug and the barge were seen to be burning brightly prior to the collision. It was also seen by radar aboard these vessels that the JAPAN POPLAR altered course at Cape Flattery, and in so doing crossed the SUDBURY ll's towline between her and her barge.

The JAPAN POPLAR's captain failed to identify the tug and tow as such, either visually or by radar. He was on radar tracking other traffic on his port forward quarter when the mate called out that there was a green light off his port bow close on. He ordered starboard helm and was almost immediately rammed by the SEASPAN 250.

The captain of the POPLAR had only been on the bridge a few minutes having been called for approaching the entrance to the Straits. It appeared that there had

SEASPAN RIGGER
The latest of the four log barges owned and operated by Seaspan International, makes a spectacular dump at the Howe Sound booming grounds.

Fully laden bulk-carrier barge SEASPAN 250
One of eight large bulk-carrier barges in the fleet, being passed by SEASPAN MONARCH (ex-Harold A. Jones). Both of these vessels were involved in separate incidents in American waters described by the author.

been great confusion on his part along with concern about the number of vessels he found in his immediate vicinity. At the time of collision the POPLAR still had her engine going full ahead. The engine had not been switched from burning heavy bunker "C" oil, to lighter diesel fuel making manouevres other than slowing down or coming to a stop impossible.

The collision gives some idea of the tremendous velocity generated by a large heavily loaded barge while under tow at about 10 knots. Our marine lawyers, Bull Housser Tupper, were very pleased with the outcome and complimented First Mate Partington on the manner he had handled matters both before the collision and during the trial.

The second case involved our tug SEASPAN MONARCH towing the 360 foot barge SEASPAN 251 fully laden with 12900 tons of limerock from Texada Island, which was destined for the Columbia Cement plant at Lake Oswego, Oregon.

I received a phone call from the Seaspan dispatch office at 0230 hours advising me that the MONARCH with her barge had been in collision with a vessel off the Columbia River, and stating that she and the barge would be in Astoria around 1100 hours.

At 0700 I contacted our legal firm, Bull Housser Tupper having booked a flight for two of us leaving Vancouver at 0930. As the accident happened in U.S. waters we contacted Bull Housser's associate law firm to meet us on arrival. I also con-

Canadian tow boat design at its best.
SEASPAN CAVALIER one of four sisterships with 1800 bhp and bollard pull of 30 short tons.
She carries 1800 feet (549 metres) of 1 3/4 inch (44.4 mm) steel wire tow line.

tacted Captain John Duke, USCG, port captain for Portland, Oregon and arranged for us all to have a joint meeting of enquiry aboard the MONARCH.

We found the barge had been rammed approximately 150 feet forward of her stern with an 80' x 16' hole in her port side where the freighter's bow had penetrated the hull through to the fore and aft bulkhead which while damaged, fortunately held, otherwise the barge would have dumped her cargo. The bow of the freighter, another Japanese, was stove in from 16 feet below her foc'sle deck to her forward collision bulkhead which fortunately also held as she was fully laden with wheat.

The SEASPAN MONARCH was able to proceed to her destination with the damaged barge. However, the Japanese vessel was unable to go any further and had to return to Portland to discharge her cargo for drydocking and major repairs.

The US Coast Guard had closed the Columbia River bar due to very recent severe storms which had made it too dangerous to cross for several days. Upon arriving off the bar the MONARCH joined other ships offshore, hove to, awaiting improved conditions to permit a reopening of the river bar.

When the opening took place, there was an accumulation of both outbound ships, and inbound ships waiting to enter. When it came to the turn of the SEASPAN MONARCH, she was instructed to proceed towards the Columbia lightship where the pilot would board her after bringing an outbound ship out.

The mate on watch aboard the MONARCH had been tracking all traffic by radar as well as visually, the night being clear with a now low ground swell. In pulling towards the lightship and pilot station he noted the ship the pilot had now leftwas on a course to pass well clear of the MONARCH and her barge and was showing red to red on his port side. The MONARCH's mate was concentrating on another ship approaching on his starboard side and altered course to give way as required. With this move completed, in looking astern he was astounded to see the outbound ship astern was now showing the lights of an overtaking vessel and was also executing a turn to starboard. Immediately he was concerned that the other vessel was too close to SEASPAN 251 for that type of turn and ran to the aft control station and turned the searchlight on to the barge which was rammed within seconds. He took tension off the winch brake so as to prevent damage to the tug and the winch.

The master of the SEASPAN MONARCH, Captain George Hovell, reported that the pilot having witnessed the collision while enroute from the Japanese ship to the MONARCH, could not understand why the ship had reversed its course as prior to leaving her he had shown her master, both visually and by radar all the positions of the vessels in the area, specifically pointing out the lights of the MONARCH and her barge and advised her master to proceed towards the Cape Lighthouse until clear of the two then alter his course for sea wishing him "bon voyage".

Tank barge SEASPAN 821
Without this tank barge and others like her there would be no gas in the pumps on the coast.

In view of the remarks of the pilot we decided to try and have a chat with him. I got his name from the pilotage, phoned him at home and he agreed to join us for dinner that night.

Upon joining us, he and I both looked at each other, as though there was some hint of recognition. In comparing jobs over the past years we found that he was a cadet aboard the PRESIDENT MADISON 45 years earlier when we transferred the appendectomy patient from the DANWOOD to his ship. Also we had met a year later in Shanghai during a visit to the Navy Y.M.C.A. while I was a cadet in the CITY OF VANCOUVER. What a small world!

He proved to be our most valuable witness in the ensuing court case over damages resulting from the collision. After a lengthy period the court decision was handed down with damages assessed against the Japanese ship of 75 per cent, with 25 per cent being awarded against the SEASPAN MONARCH.

Aboard the Japanese ship it was found that the captain had left the bridge for his room prior to seeing his ship clear of the close traffic and setting his seagoing course. A mate and quartermaster were on watch and a lookout had not been posted. Apparently the mate became confused and made a turn to go astern of the barge without realising there was insufficient clearance to enable him to complete the turn with his heavily laden vessel.

GLOBAL AMBITION
Four Seaspan tugs assisting the fire damaged, fully loaded bulk-carrier through the Lions Gate. SEASPAN REGENT leading with SEASPAN COMMODORE on the ship's starboard side. These two tugs each with a maximum power output of 6325 BHP are the most powerful in the fleet.

The mate of the SEASPAN MONARCH was faulted for not sounding "U" on his whistle, thus signalling to the freighter, "you are standing into danger", when he saw the vessel start the turn towards his barge.

Seaspan decided to appeal the decision, considering that the whistle would not have been heard without a lookout man being outside the wheelhouse of the Japanese ship as required. Also there could be no excuse on a clear night for those on watch not seeing the brightly burning lights on the barge which had previously been pointed out by the pilot. Apparently they could not have been keeping an efficient radar track or plot; in other words the watchkeeping practices aboard the Japanese freighter were deficient on several counts.

The appeal court decision found in favour of Seaspan with a revision from their assessment down by ten per cent to 15%. which was well worth while considering the close to $2.5 million involved in the joint damages and lost time. This decision indicates once again how important strict watchkeeping practices are, with full compliance with the International Rules of the Road for preventing collisions at sea.

On a more personal note I found that the demands of the job and the heavy travelling back and forth at times seven days a week, between Boundary Bay and Vancouver became too stressful. More than that my hours tended to be governed by vessel arrivals, regardless of the time, which had to have my attention. We had purchased this property with a view to our retirement, but after a short time of this routine we regretfully decided that we should sell, which we did, and then purchased a condominium in North Vancouver. This worked out well in relation to my job, but then we felt the urge for something else of a more recreational nature, so purchased a 21' cruiser which got us out on weekends into Howe Sound and around the Gulf Islands to enjoy swimming, fishing, crabbing or just plain lazing around. I had been sailing the coast for many years, but always with the objective of going from one point to another by the most economical routing possible. On many occasions I had been intrigued as to what this inlet or that bay might be like. One could hear all sorts of good things about them from yachtsman friends, or find out details in the B.C. Coast Pilot or simply picture them as one looked at a chart, but they remained forever elusive until we had our own boat to explore at our leisure.

Later this boat was replaced by a larger 26 foot vessel with greater range and better facilities on board. Whereas basically the first boat was little more than a weekender, the new vessel was a full livaboard giving us a better chance of enjoying an extended holiday. During 1980, my health had not been too good, having been affected by past injuries, but with my seniority I was now able to get a little extra time off more frequently.

We explored Jervis Inlet in detail and then came through the Skookumchuck Rapids to take a close look at beautiful Sechelt Inlet, and in the process got to know anchorages and tie up spots as well as local people. Previously we had been able to obtain permission to tie our boat up at the company's booming ground at Twin Creeks between Gibsons and Port Mellon, which enabled us to quickly travel by car on the ferry in order to reach the boat. We did the same in Porpoise Bay, Sechelt, leaving the boat there and going back and forth by car. We were so taken with the area that quite soon the idea of making our home in Sechelt took hold and we purchased our first home in West Sechelt, selling our North Vancouver condominium at a speed which surprised us. Commuting would take a lot of extra time

The biggest bulk-carrier in the fleet.
SEASPAN 270, 16,000 tons deadweight capacity at sea with a full load of lumber destined for the U.S.

so Eunice would spend her time up there and I arranged for a sleeping room in North Vancouver from Mondays through to Fridays.

I was now able to get a decent vacation each year, something which when you are at sea is always subject to the vaguaries and demands of service afloat. Quite apart from that attitudes are different, the average seagoing man being more content to enjoy his home with his wife and family during his time off. When one comes to a job ashore as I did, the idea of getting out on the water takes on a new dimension particularly if, like me, there is a lingering nostalgia for the earlier years at sea. We usually tried to get away for the last week in June and first two weeks in July and this gave us a nice opportunity for a really good long cruise with our larger boat. As I mentioned several chapters back, Eunice is a natural seawoman and boat handler, and was fully capable of taking the wheel for long stretches, which certainly added to my enjoyment. To be truthful every boating couple should be fully conversant with their boat rather than one of them ending up helpless when an emergency occurs.

This fact was so important to us in our northern travels as once we got into the maze of islands north of Campbell River and Powell River, the area known by towboatmen as the "jungles", we would be days at times without seeing another vessel, and radio contact was difficult to impossible in some areas on account of the high mountains which made transmission extremely difficult. We would always take the inside route to Forward Harbour via the Yaculta rapids, Green Point Rapids and the

"Flagship of the fleet"
SEASPAN COMMODORE slowly moving with a giant log barge at the end of the towline.

Whirlpool Rapids. A night might be spent at Forward Harbour, then weather permitting we would exit out through Sunderland Channel into Johnstone Straits and then carry on up the straits to Broken Islands at the entrance to Havanna Channel and thus enter our jungle holiday world of peace and quiet with our widlife neighbours all around us.

My health started to act up again, so my doctor gave me a letter to the company suggesting that I be put on lighter duties in a less stressful job, so after talking it over with senior management, who could see that I was going backwards in this regard, decided to put me on long term disability until I slid into retirement about one year later. Life became a good deal more relaxed as for all practical purposes I was now retired, even if unofficially, and for the first time in my working life I was not under the pressure of working to a schedule. When 65 was reached and retirement became official, the company invited Eunice and me to a retirement luncheon, with all my shoreside associates present. They presented me with a magnificent coffee table with a genuine ship's steering wheel built into it. This was specially made at Vancouver Shipyards, Seaspan's shipbuilding and repair associate. It incorporates beautiful craftsmanship and sits proudly in our living room as a memento of my years with Seaspan and its predecessor Island Tug & Barge. Accompanying this was a very nice cheque from Seaspan to top off a wonderful send-off.

"Home Base for port captains"
Headquarters of both Seaspan International and Vancouver Shipyards, the authors last port of call prior to retirement.

All told I served as a towboat master for 24 years in vessels of Vancouver Barge Transportation, Dola Towing, Island Tug & Barge and Seaspan. On coming ashore I did a further 13 years of shoreside duty in Island Tug & Barge, and Seaspan. I must say that in retirement I had plenty of opportunity to reflect on the very large fleet of tugs and barges which make up the Seaspan fleet. The company has kept everything that it owns in top condition and always up to date in terms of its technical requirements.

I am sure there are crews around who are up to the same high standard as that upon which Seaspan insists, but I know there are none better. From the initial faltering steps when VanIsle Tug & Barge came into being as a result of the merger between its founding components, it has become a first class major international transportation concern, with its own traditions of quality and service, a solid core of tremendous people on shore from top management down to the secretaries who look after so many essential elements of the management machine. When Vancouver Shipyards staff is added to that of Seaspan it is certainly now the largest employer on the Vancouver waterfront and as such a tremendous asset to the Port of Vancouver.

Epilogue

Finished with Engines

Before ringing off "Finished with Engines" certain events form vivid memories of my other consuming interest. The first of these concerns my formation, and being in charge of a trumpet band in the 5th B.C. Coast Brigade, Royal Canadian Artillery in Victoria when our greatest honour was being the duty band at the Parliament Buildings on Armistice Day. Our entire trumpet section sounded the "Last Post" and "Reveille" in perfect unison, and I believe this was the first time that these calls had been sounded by other than a single trumpeter or bugler at these services.

The other big event was the reforming of the "Lonsdale" Sea Cadet Corps Band in North Vancouver almost thirty years later, when it was increased in size and new band instruments obtained during my service with it.

Just as momentous was the successful acquisition of our own vessel which became a seagoing training ship. The ship was an ex-tug, with an overall length of 75 feet powered by a 230 h.p. Union diesel. She was the MALASPINA STRAITS ex CHEERFUL, owned by Straits Towing and had been decommissioned and tied up for some time.

I had approached Senator Stan McKeen who had been my employer when I worked for Straits Towing Ltd, when it was known as Standard Towing Company. He offered us the vessel for the nominal sum of one dollar, and immediately after transfer formalities were completed she was registered to "The Lonsdale Sea Cadet Officers Association" which we had formed because the Navy League would not assume responsibility for her.

With hard work by the cadets and their parents, together with volunteers from the Deck and Engineroom departments of the Marine Unions. The vessel was thoroughly cleaned up, painted grey and all engine room facilities and the engines made operable. The marine industries community as a whole donated all our needs and services as we required them to make the now re-named STRAITS CADET into a seagoing training ship as shown in the picture of her backing away from her berth in North Vancouver on her inaugural trip with all our guest donors, along with R.C.N. and Navy league officials.

Through the days of refitting and rccommissioning the donations of supplies and services were unbelievable, including paint, drydockings, fuel and lubricating oils for our annual requirements, repairs, a lifeboat, life rings, belts and buoys, winch removal along with extension of the house aft to enlarge the galley and messroom, radiotelephone, intercom systems and radar. It was heartening to see the way in which the marine community rallied around this worthwhile project and gave so readily.

The steamship inspection officer whom I knew volunteered to give the vessel a thorough annual inspection. This was not an official requirement because the STRAITS CADET was now registered as a yacht, but was a very good precaution considering the large numbers we could expect to have on board. One major item

Diesel Tug MALASPINA STRAITS
Through the kindness of Senator S.S. McKeen this veteran of the Straits Towing fleet became the STRAITS CADET.

Training Ship STRAITS CADET
The former MALASPINA STRAITS aquired from Straits Towing for one dollar!

"At ease"
Lonsdale Sea Cadet Corps Band readying for a march.

arose when we were advised that a new tailshaft could be necessary a year later. I approached Dafoe's a Coal Harbour machine shop with whom I had dealt before and they gave me their cost price for material which we raised during the year. Upon completion of the shaft we were advised that labour costs had all been donated by their employees.

When away from the dock STRAITS CADET was always in charge of a certificated master and engineer with one of three trained cadet crews from LONSDALE. The vessel was made available to all Sea Cadet and Wrenette corps, free of charge for training cruises during which teaching in all areas of seamanship and engineroom duties, cooking and galley work, signals, navigation, radio, radar, steering, standing watches at sea, and in port dealing with bends, hitches and splicing.

This project which had been helped by so many people came to an end when the Navy League made it impossible for us to carry on with our vessel and we were forced to sell her. It was a great pity that such a worthwhile project had to close down and it is sometimes very hard to figure out how the official mind works!

The "Lonsdale Sea Cadet Corps Band" received many cups following participation in competitive parades, several being in the Seattle Annual Torch Light Parade. After the second cup, to the delight of all band members, and years later my grandchildren, I was presented in front of the whole corps with a "Davy Crockett" coonskin cap as shown in the picture within the text. We also attended May 24th parades in Sechelt, being transported from Gibsons to Sechelt by school bus, but when the STRAITS CADET was commissioned we were able to travel directly to the Sechelt government dock in Traill Bay.

My elder son Dan became drum major of the cadet band and in the family group picture he can be seen in his chief petty officers uniform, with our youngest

Lieut. Governor Clarence Wallace escorted by the author, inspecting the Lonsdale Sea Cadet Corps band in the late 1950's.

"Davey Crockett"
The author displays tropies, including the cap, won by the Lansdale Sea Cadet Corps Band at Seattle.

"A Navy Family"
L to R Chief Petty Officer Dan Wilson, Lieutenant Ted Wilson, Wrenette Sub-Lieut. Eunice Wilson, and Cadet Ted Wilson Jr.

son Ted as a junior cadet. Proudly completing the picture are us two parents, sub-lieutenant Eunice of the Wrenettes, and myself as the lieutenant in charge.

In these modern times when so much emphasis is placed on the dis-functionalism of modern families, and the many reasons for family breakdowns, including in the case of seafaring men the fact that they are frequently away for lengthy periods, I want to acknowledge that we as a family were fortunate in avoiding this. Much credit goes to Eunice who not only was a full time mother, but very frequently surrogate father as well, particularly during our sons' most impressionable years. Neither Dan or Ted ever gave us any cause for concern as they went through childhood, and into manhood and that alone is a cause for great satisfaction on our part.

During the later years of Dola Towing and Pacific Towing, both sons loved to help out during overhaul periods and worked right along with everyone else in cleaning boilers and tubes, scraping, painting, and polishing brass while the wartime grey was removed.

Dan put himself through U.B.C. while working his summers aboard the Canadian Pacific passenger ships. He started as a dishwasher and worked his way up to steward aboard the cruise ship PRINCESS PATRICIA, prior to completing his Master's degree in Education. He went into teaching and is still busily engaged in that profession.

During his school days, Ted worked in service stations, until completing high school after which he joined Island Tug & Barge as a deckhand. He served four years in major vessels of the fleet including my two favourites SEA LION and LLOYD B. GORE while I was master in them.

"Happily Retired"
Ted and Eunice Wilson, celebrating their 50th anniversary at their home in Sechelt, B.C..

Ted in meeting his love and becoming engaged decided that the sea was going to keep him away from the sort of home life he wanted, for too lengthy periods of time. He left his sea career and went into sales where he worked himself up into the management position he holds today.

Our two sons and their families have been a source of great pride and satisfaction to us and the latest generation of the family are now making their own choices of career after graduating from U.B.C. This happy recollection has only been marred by one event, and we remember with much love our promising 16-year old grandson who tragically lost his life in a traffic accident with three school mates while on their way to a basketball game at Princeton.

Now having been retired for 8 years, and very happily married for 50 years I have wonderful memories of my working years, including past ships and shipmates along with all those business associates and friends that I have been fortunate enough to know. Since retirement I have maintained contact with many old working friends and made a lot of new ones as the result of addressing service clubs and other groups on maritime matters. One last memory I must recall, when on "full line, full away", that is, when we were almost always under way with a barge in tow, concerns my then 6 year-old son Dan, on the occasion when I took him on a trip with me for the first time.

We had left Vancouver with a loaded Canadian Pacific railcar barge in tow for Nanoose Bay, with Dan sound asleep in my bunk where I joined him after clearing First Narrows. Breaking day outside Nanoose Bay the mate called me, and Dan woke up. He scrambled out of the bunk, and went to the cabin door which was ajar, to the boat deck, and the next thing I knew he turned around eyes agog and gasped,

"Dad, do you know there is a big barge following us",

"I hope so son, I sure hope so". I replied with a chuckle.

After all if that barge was not following on our towline I would surely have had real problems, with a run-away barge to look for.

Finished with engines!

Photo Acknowledgements

The authors are indebted to Mr. Leonard McCann, curator of the Vancouver Maritime Museum, and Mrs. Debbie Tardiff of Seaspan International Ltd. in obtaining the use of the following photographs, numbered against the names of their organizations.

Allen Aerial Photos Ltd.	157.
Heal collection	25, 112 top.
Seaspan International Ltd.	143, 146, 147, 148, 149, 150, 151, 152, 153, 155, 156.
Vancouver Maritime Museum	19 top, 23, 33, 34, 37 top, 42 bottom, 50, 61, 84, 85, 86, 106, 120 top, 123, 138.

All other photographs are from the James E. Wilson personal collection.

CORDILLERA PUBLISHING COMPANY specializes in the publishing and production of quality books dealing with maritime history, commercial shipping, commercial fisheries and fish and shellfish farming, ship and boat-building techniques and history, and the marine industries generally. Marine, civil and military aviation are of similar interest.

CORDILLERA would be interested in hearing from authors, or writers in these fields. In the first instance please contact us by mail at the address shown below, enclosing a stamped addressed return envelope. All enquiries will receive a response and a copy of our writers guidelines:

CORDILLERA PUBLISHING COMPANY
8415 Granville Street
Dept. 46
Vancouver, B.C.
Canada. V6P 4Z9